This book is dedicated to my younger self
and all the other young Black men who experience a similar plight..
The world is yours.

To everyone else... **Welcome to Steel City.**

Welcome To Steel City

By EJ Nunley

Hip Hop Literature
11101 Frankstown Raad
Suite 500
Pittsburgh, PA 15235
(412) 968-6041
https://www.hiphoplitpublishing.com/contact

Chapter 1

J abar "Body" Jones was born July 4, 1989 in Pittsburgh, PA at Magee Women's Hospital. He was born in the height of the crack epidemic and would've been a crack baby, but his mother was a heroin addict instead. Her name was Robin Janice Jones. She was twenty-three years old when she gave birth to Jabar. His father? He never knew his father,... not even his name.

Robin would never mention a word to Jabar about his father. Being very young and inquisitive, he would often ask his mother questions about the identity of his father. *Like, what is his name? What does he look like? How did you meet my dad?* All of the typical things a child may want to know about their father. Jabar would yield negative results for his inquiries. After a while, he learned to stop asking.

Jabar was under the impression that his raise didn't know the identity of his father. The word *raise* is Pittsburgh's terminology. It's slang used in the place of mom or grandma. Your grandma is known as your *grandraise*. That's as far as it goes in the hood because nine out of ten people are raised by either their mother or grandmother. Daddies were nowhere to be found and came too few and far in between. Body never met any of his friends' dads. There was a good chance that they had never met their fathers either.

Robin had one other child, a girl named Jasmine. Unfortunately, Jasmine never had an opportunity to meet her father either. Robin, however, did know his identity. His name was Fred Johnson and he was a notorious stick-up kid back in the day. When Robin was pregnant with Jasmine, Fred was shot and killed by the police as he attempted to escape with the cash he robbed from Mellon Bank.

Jasmine was five years younger than Jabar. It was his responsibility to take care of her being as their mother spent the majority of her time in a shooting gallery. Jasmine was Jabar's life. He vowed that he would provide for her and protect her at all cost.

Jasmine was 11 years old. Body had not only been a big brother to her, but a father as well for the entirety of their young lives. Jasmine was a pretty, little, light-skinned girl with long, thick, jet-black hair that she usually wore in two pigtails. She was very smart and she excelled in school academically. She was quiet and usually kept to herself. Besides having Body, the only other person she had, who she could count on was her grandraise, Mama Jones.

Mama Jones was a strong black woman with old school morals and values. She was what some might call a *country woman*. She was born in Birmingham, Alabama sometime in the 1950's. She ran away from home at the tender age of 17 in order to escape Jim Crow. Also, to rid herself of the horrific memories of a detrimental and degrading act committed against her.

While walking home late one afternoon, she was approached by three white men in an old Chevy pickup truck. The men proceeded to taunt and nag her, but she ignored them and continued to walk along.

That was until she had to walk past a wooded area. Back in those days white men considered it a "rite of passage" to conquer a black woman. It was a prerequisite of sorts for leaving childhood and entering into manhood for this particular group.

This being the case, the men decided that they wanted to have some fun with the *poor little nigger girl*. They even convinced themselves that she would, somehow, enjoy it. Armed with the liquid courage that Bourbon brings, they all jumped out of the truck and attacked her. She put up one hell of a fight, but her struggles proved to be futile. She wasn't any match for three grown men. They dragged her kicking and screaming into the woods and commenced to rape her one by one. The end result was a pregnancy. Being raised as a Christian and having devout parents, she didn't believe in abortions. She was faced with the toughest decision of her young life. To save face and avoid public scrutiny and humiliation from having a baby out of wedlock, she packed her bags with the $200 she managed to save and boarded a Greyhound bus en route to Pittsburgh, PA.

When she arrived in Pittsburgh, she didn't know a soul. She chose her destination because it was the furthest she could go from her hometown within her budget. She was confident that she would make a way for herself and her child with the assistance of government aid and an under the table job. The job would be as a barmaid at Lena's Bar on Wylie Avenue. After seven months on the job, she gave birth to Robin.

The trauma of the rape had a negative psychological impact on Mama Jones and affected Robin just the same, if not more. The knowledge of being a product of rape was too much for Robin to endure. Growing up in an era when heroin was the drug of choice and readily available to the public, Robin chose to indulge in an effort to drown her sorrows and soothe her depression.

Mama Jones tried religiously to instill a sense of pride and education in her daughter in hopes to raise her self esteem. She did the same for her grandchildren. Robin may have slipped from her grasp, but Mama Jones was hell bent on making sure that neither Jabar nor Jasmine would go down that path. She was adamant about making sure that those kids would always have two things to carry with them throughout life, morals and education. She felt that it was especially important for Jabar.

Being a young, black, man-child growing up in America, he would need those things the most. Since Mama Jones always expressed the importance of education, she decided it would be best to be proactive. Being an avid reader herself, she would educate Body on his "real" history. She was well aware that the curriculums in the public schools were shot to shit. She did everything in her power to give him what she felt he needed most, a sense of self and knowledge of his history.

Body could remember vividly the way his grandraise would say, *"Jabar you have to have a sense of self and knowledge of where you came from to know where you're going, baby."*

The older Body got, the more he believed that was a croc of shit. How could he have such pride about where he came from and no one had taken the liberty of telling him the identity of his father? But, no matter how he felt, he wouldn't disrespect his grandraise. Mama Jones' stern ways paid off in some capacity because he excelled in school. Not only athletically, but academically. Body normally took heed to the teachings of his grandraise. Although, growing up and coming into his own, he began to develop ideologies that didn't coincide with hers. Being a young hustler, he believed that there wasn't any sense in having money and not knowing what to do with it. *This was* the main reason he paid such close attention in school. He could hear his grandraise's voice in his head, *"a fool and his money shall soon part."* She *loved* to quote scriptures. He got it. Body understood that he needed to learn how to hold onto what little he had.

Despite his extra-curricular activities, Body managed to maintain a 3.5 grade point average throughout his years at Schenley High School. Since freshman year, he had been hustling on the same block. Arriving in high school was a totally different ball game. He would need to get himself some gear or he wouldn't be attending. At the previous school, all he had to do was to keep his sneakers clean and he was able to get by. There wouldn't be any getting by like that at Schenley. He would be the laughing-stock of the entire school and surely he couldn't catch the attention of all the pretty girls he liked, if he was wearing rags. But, he didn't have to worry about that too much because there were plenty of crackheads in the hood, so he was sure to stay *fly*.

Besides that, Body loved to play basketball. He was the captain of the varsity team for the Schenley Spartans. He was the starting number 2 shooting guard. At 16 years old, he measured in at 6'1", 170 pounds. His skin complexion was light brown. His wavy hair was cut into a Caesar with tapered sides. He had a lean muscular build with hardly an ounce of body fat. He loved to workout and a lot of people, mostly women, believe that was where his moniker "Body" stemmed from, his physique. Anybody who's somebody already knew the truth. And the truth was that Body earned his name by putting in work.

In a city like Pittsburgh, putting in work was the norm for any up and coming young hustler who had plans to continue his rise in the game. This city was the epitome of a "dog eat dog" world. It was the straight up jungle! It didn't matter if the jungle consisted of trees or skyscrapers, you still had to live by it's law, which was "bite or be bitten". Body chose to bite. He had a similar approach when it came to the drug game. The way he saw it was, you were either a smoker or a slinger, a boss or runner, a hustler or fiend.

His grandraise looked down on the drug game and would verbally express her disdain about it. She would often say things to Body like, *"I don't want you out there selling that poison. You kids out there killing your own kind, your own community!"*

Body's perspective was different. Since he was a child, he had always heard about the ills of the drug trade and how it was responsible for destroying Black communities. Whenever drug dealers were mentioned by his grandraise, her friends, or members of her church congregation, they were spoken of as if they were sellouts and guilty of treason.

It was almost as if drug dealers were the biggest problem plaguing *Black America* and without them the community's problems would suddenly disappear. Body's philosophies were completely different and his views were shaped by his own experiences as opposed to someone else's opinions or traditions.

His experience in the drug game and connection to the Black community gave him an in-depth, vivid view into the lives and psyche of those that he came in contact with on a daily basis. The way that Body saw things was that everyone had an addiction and through those addictions, people selected a drug of choice. Some addicts chose heroin, cocaine, crack, weed, ecstasy, or alcohol. Some were addicted to over the counter prescription pills, painkillers or syrup. Then, there were others who were addicts of gambling or sex. They were willing to give up or risk everything seeking the thrill or rush of a bet.

The rest had some of the weirdest sexual fantasies and appetites or the most bizarre fetishes known to man. You see, Body understood that people needed distractions to help occupy their time. So, they didn't have to deal with their own realities or the real world. They needed something to help them cope with the harsh realities of life. They weren't strong enough to handle these conditions on their own. So as long as these people need substances to help them cope with life, Body would continue to sell crack!

He could often be heard saying things like, *"It's supply and demand baby! America taught me this shit! This is capitalism at its motherfucking best!"* Body knew that at the end of the day, it was all about the power of the almighty dollar. Being semi-politically conscious, he would often twist the facts of events or circumstances to fit his own personal views.

Chapter 2

While sitting in the passenger seat of an older model Chevy Lumina, Body spoke his mind to his right-hand man, Psycho.

"Think about this shit going on out here, Psych. The government don't give a fuck about these muthafuckas out here smoking crack, getting high and shit. They just want a fucking cut. And since America won't stand for them legalizing the shit because it's supposed to be immoral." He said using his fingers to make quotations and mocking the word.

"They get their cut by putting our black asses in jail. If niggas pay taxes on all that crack they be slinging in the hood, it would be all good. That shit would be legal."

Body paused as he took a long drag from the blunt of sour diesel. He inhaled deeply. He held it for a moment and then slowly exhaled. As the clouds of weed smoke quickly filled the interior of the car, Body continued his philosophy.

"Did you know that alcohol used to be illegal in this country, too?" asked Body.

"Yeah, I know about that shit." said Psycho in a weed-induced haze.

"You see that shit is legal now and it's state regulated. So, they getting all the money. If they can't tax it, you can't have it. That's all it's about. That's why they won't legalize this shit here." Body said referring to the weed that they were smoking.

"This shit should be legal, already. Fucking scientists already proved that there's no possible way to overdose on it."

The full effect of the weed had taken over Body at that point and he was in a deep zone. He got that way anytime he smoked some good weed.

"You know what this shit reminds me of?" He said more to himself than Psycho. "Reminds me of Frank White in the *King of New York*. If a nickel bag is sold in the park, I want in!"

Both friends erupted in laughter as Body impersonated the actor from the famous movie. Psycho liked hearing Body talk like that. For such a young guy, he had a unique way of seeing the world.

Psycho, who's real name was Raymond Brown, was Body's best friend. They grew up together on The Hill. The Hill (short for Hill District) was one of the city's most densely populated communities. It was mostly comprised of housing projects. Both, Psycho and Body, were from Burrows Street Projects in the 100-block area. Burrows Street was a long residential street that stretched the span of a half mile in length. There were three story project buildings on each side. Well at least that's the way that Burrows Street used to look. That was before the city began knocking down the project complexes around the Hill District and replacing them with townhomes. That was before gentrification. Along with the new townhomes, came a set of strict policies and rules in an effort to drive Blacks out of the inner city.

The first project to be torn down was none other than Robinson Court. It was better known as R.C. In the mid 1990's, there was a story reported about R.C. on the infamous program *60 minutes*. They called R.C. by it's other well known moniker, "Crack County". It

11

was easy to get rich in a place like R.C. where kilos of crack were sold on a daily basis. If you couldn't get paid in a place like R.C., you were worthless as a hustler.

Along with R.C., the Hill District was home to many other projects and they all contained big money making potential. There was Waring Court, which like many of the other projects on the Hill was one way in and one way out. That was just fine for the hustlers because it made it easier to spot the police coming and to direct traffic. Waring Court was constructed in the shape of a half circle with project buildings lined up along its border and a few courts in the middle. It wasn't a big project by any stretch of the imagination. Because of all the rampant crime there, including rape, robbery, drug dealing, shooting and killing, it was dubbed as the "Mad Circle".

A lot of money flowed through "The Mad". It was a hustler's dream. But, like Burrows Street and R.C., the Mad Circle was brought to its knees as well. It was beginning to seem as though the city was attempting to bring the entire hood down. In 2003, yet another project was torn down. This time it was Whiteside Road, better known as "Weed Side".

Despite all of these seemingly hurtful setbacks, the Hill still held plenty of earning potential. And was home to quite a few project complexes that remained standing. There was Elmore Square, better known as "G Block", Somers, Chauncey, Frances, and of course Bentley Drive. The townhouses that now replace Burrows street are now known as Oak Hill.

Both Body and Psycho's raises resided in an Oak Hill townhouse. They lived three houses apart and had been inseparable since grade school. Year after year, they walked to school together making plans for the future and dreamt of being rich. They had no *real* knowledge of the game; they were just down for whatever. They learned the ropes as they went along, trial and error.

Body and Psycho learned a lot at young ages. They were far more advanced than their peers, despite the learning curves. They started out pitching in to buy a half-kilo of coke that was cooked up and distributed on the block in fives, tens, and twenties. They had always split everything 50/50, including the Chevy Lumina that they shared to make moves and get from point A to point B.

They pulled late night shifts on the block together watching each other's back. Then, they would retire to the crib so they could get up and go to school the next morning. Living only three houses apart was convenient for the both of them. They would go in the house, get a short couple hours of sleep and wake up the following morning for school. This was the usual routine for a while, but it slowly began to change. They still continued to pull the same long hours on the block together. Go home together and awake early the next morning tired as hell from the previous night's events. Then, head toward school. The difference in routine began once they arrived at Schenley.

Psycho being the driver would pull to the entrance of the school and say "Aight B, I'll holla at you, later."

"Whatchu mean you gonna holla at me, later? What you about to do, nigga?" asked Body.

"I'm about to go down Bentley and get right." said Psycho.

"You ain't going to school?" Body asked.

"Nah, not today, Ike." said Psycho. This slowly, but surely started to become the norm. .

***

Psycho held different opinions than Body, when it came to school. He didn't believe that it was a necessity to go to school, anymore. It was 2006. He was at the end of his junior year. He figured that he already knew everything, he needed to know. So, when he was confronted by Body about why he wasn't going to school, anymore. He was ready to reply.

"Yo Psych, what's good with school, Ike?" asked Body.

Ike was Pittsburgh's terminology, or more like the Hill District's terminology. Only people who were from the Hill said *Ike*. The word has been around for as long as Body could remember. It originated when a popular guy from the Hill named Ikey Dawg died a sudden death. From that day forth, the name Ike was the terminology used in remembrance of and as the equivalent of saying *my nigga*.

"Whatchu mean, what's good with school?" asked Psych.

"I mean, this year is already over with and we only got one more year to graduate, my nigga. It don't really make no sense not to finish, now. Don't fuck up now, Ike." said Body.

"Nah, I aint fucking up. I'm just doing me. Honestly, I could care less about all that school shit or graduating. All of that shit ain't for me no more, Ike. The way I see this shit is, why waste my time going to school? Taking up all dem hours out of my day. Trying to get a diploma? Some bullshit ass piece of paper that I ain't never gonna use. I definitely ain't working for nobody, getting paid some low ass wages. So, that job shit is out. Plus, while niggas are sitting in them classes, listening to all that bullshit. I'm outchea making more money than those teachers. So, what the fuck they gonna teach me? I already know how to read nigga and as long as I can count this money, I'm good. I ain't got no plans to go to nobody's college, my nigga."

"Coach Mike was asking about you the other day." Body interjected.

"Yeah well, ya ass don't be going to no practice, either" Psycho responded.

"Yeah, but at least I'm still going to school and my ass *is* gonna graduate." said Body. Psycho was unmoved.

Psycho was skilled when it came to basketball. It was the hood's favorite pastime. So, most niggas who came from the Hill could usually ball. Standing tall at only 5'8" on a good day, Psycho's height didn't hurt his production at all. Psycho was a hell of a point guard. Anything he lacked in height; he more than made up for in heart. He was the starting point guard for the Spartans, until his attendance dropped too low for him to make eligibility to play. Anytime, Psycho was in school, it was more about showing off than learning.

Psycho was short for a man by all standards. His complexion was dark brown and his build was stocky. He wore his shoulder-length hair in stylish braids. He always wore the latest fashion and loved to turn the hallways of school into a fashion show. Psycho received his moniker the same way Body did by putting in work on the Hill.

However, Psycho was much more of a loose cannon than Body could ever be.

Chapter 3

O ne day Psycho was looking for a guy named Tye. Tye owed him $450 from a half ounce of crack that Psycho fronted him on consignment. Tye was from Chauncey Projects. Naturally, that's where he hustled. So, Psycho knew exactly where to find him.

Dressed to brave the winter weather, Psycho was wearing all black from head to toe. He decided that he would visit Chauncey to check up on Tye and his money. When Psycho reached Chauncey, he found Tye posted up in the first hallway of the "Corporate Court". Niggas called it Corporate Court because of the large sums of cash that flowed through there. Tye was in the hallway hustling. He had his girlfriend with him, some little chicken head named Keisha. Keisha was cute as far as looks go. She was light-skinned, short hair, and had a fat ass. But, she was a *jump off*. Psycho knew her from school.

When Psycho walked up the steps, Tye was automatically startled because he was caught off guard. He was too busy gripping on Keisha's booty to be paying attention to anything else. Tye stammered as he tried to regain his composure and play things cool.

"Oh, wha wha what's good, Psych?" Tye managed to say as he extended his hand for dap. Psycho, rudely, ignored the friendly gesture.

Keisha spoke as well. "Hey, Ray." Psycho ignored her too and confronted Tye.

"You know what's good, nigga! Where my change?"

"Damn, you ain't gotta say it like that, Ike. Why you trippin' about a couple punk ass dollars?" said Tye.

"Nigga, fuck that! You've been ducking me for two weeks now! You slowing up shit I gotta do and I want interest, nigga".

"Interest?" Tye replied in a confused manner.

"Yeah, nigga. Interest! Additional money. You know what the fuck I'm saying. You was been supposed to pay me. You think I'm stupid, nigga? You out here flipping my change. Now, I want my cut. I want $900."

Feeling embarrassed in front of Keisha, Tye attempted to save face and pop fly. "Nigga, I ain't paying no fucking interest! Fuck you think you is, nigga? As a matter of fact, I ain't paying shit! You ain't even from up here, nigga. So, you better leave while you still can Ike, nephs"

That was as far as Tye had gotten with his tirade. Gripping the .357 that was concealed inside the pocket of his *Northface*, Psycho shot Tye through the pocket of his coat. The sound of the tre-pound barking was muffled by the coat's heavy insulation of feathers. Tye fell to his knees in agonizing pain, clutching his stomach and bleeding into his palms.

"You shot me, Ike." winced Tye.

Psycho, then pulled the nickel-plated .357 from his pocket and pointed it at Tye's head, "Shut the fuck up, nigga! You was just tough a minute ago." Keisha stood still watching, wide-eyed with fear and shock.

"Bitch, what the fuck is you looking at?" Psycho yelled at Keisha.

Keisha fearfully replied, "Chill Ray, I ain't got nothing to do with that."

"Nah, fuck that. Come over here and get my money out this nigga's pockets." said Psycho.

Keisha did what she was told and immediately began rifling through all of Tye's pockets. She quickly located the wad of cash she saw earlier that day. Tye had been flashing his knot trying to impress her. She handed the money to Psycho.

Psycho looked through the bills and estimated between $1,100 to $1,200. He put the money in his pocket then asked Tye, "Where the fuck is that work at?"

"It's in the mailbox." Tye replied.

"Keisha, get that fucking key out of his pocket." demanded Psycho. Keisha removed the key to the mailbox from Tye's pocket. She attempted to hand it over to Psycho.

"Nah, go open that shit." said Psycho.

Keisha went over and opened the mailbox and brought all of its contents back to Psycho, which included 2 ounces of crack, a quarter ounce of weed, a Glock .40 and a small handheld digital scale.

"What the fuck you doing with your gun in the mailbox, stupid?" asked Psycho.

"Alright, you got everything just leave, Ray." said Keisha timidly.

"Nah, fuck that. I ain't about to have beef with this nigga, when I can get this shit over with right now." Psycho responded.

With that being said, he pointed the .357 at Tye's head as Tye's wide teary eyes stared at him in fear. Keisha chimed in with one last attempt, "Ray, you're crazy!"

He turned his head and looked her square in the eyes and replied, "Nah, bitch. I'm Psycho!"

Boom! Boom! Boom!

The .357 barked loudly. Chunks of Tye's skull jumped from the back of his head and landed on everything in the hallway, including the face of a sobbing terrified Keisha. Psycho pocketed the Glock .40, the scale and weed. He tossed the $1200 to Keisha and fled the scene.

When it came to the game or putting in work, Body was more thoughtful and far more meticulous than Psycho. He would plan everything first. He had more patience, which enabled him to wait and think things through and make better decisions. Those decisions were usually right for him. He dreaded the day that he may be caught red-handed for murder. He knew that, if he ran into the police after a murder that there was a very strong likelihood that, he would spend the rest of his life in prison. Never to see the light of day, again.

In Pennsylvania ,if you are given *life*, an *"L"*, an *"elbow"* ...it means forever. There is no possibility of parole. With this in mind, Body would always carry extra clips of ammunition with him, whenever he went on a hit. If push came to shooting, Body knew that he would hold court in the streets. He was certain that Psycho felt the same way.

So, he couldn't understand for the life of him why Psych' would take such unnecessary risks at times.

For a measly $450, Body would've charged the Tye situation to the game. He would've gotten Tye out of his life for cheap. He would *never* have given him shit else, again. He would spend $450 on a pair of sneakers at the *Gucci* store. Body wasn't about to kill Tye or anybody else for that matter over sneaker money. All of the negative possibilities that could arise, afterward, wasn't worth it. Psycho, however, would kill a nigga strictly because of the principle and deal with the consequences later. His motto was *"squeeze first, ask questions last."*

***

The summer had officially arrived. Body and Psycho succeeded in passing the 11th grade, despite all of Psycho's absent days. It didn't take much to graduate from the city's public schools. Both young men celebrated their 17th birthdays in the height of summer. Body was a Cancer. His birthday fell on the Fourth of July. Psycho was a Gemini. His birthday was on June 19th. True to tradition, they celebrated their birthdays together, this year like every other year, since they were toddlers.

Ring! Ring! Ring!

"Hello?" a young female voice answered.

"What's up, Jas? Where ya brother at?"

"Oh. Hi Ray. He's in his room. Hold on for a second."

Jasmine knocked on the door and waited for Body to respond, before she entered. After a moment of waiting with no response, she began to bang on the door.

"Jabar? Raymond is on the phone!" said Jasmine.

"Come in!" Body replied. Jasmine entered the room and looked around at the mess that had amassed.

"You need to clean this room up. It looks like a pigsty in here."

There were clothes thrown all around the room with shoes, boots and shoe boxes scattered about the floor. On the nightstand, there were mounds of blunt guts, a half smoked blunt and a few roaches in the ashtray.

"Why don't you clean it for me?"

"Why don't you pay me?" Jasmine responded with a smirk on her face. She tossed Body the cordless phone and left the room.

"Hello."

"What's the drill, Ike? I see Jas is putting the squeeze on you, even on your birthday!" said Psycho, causing him and Body to laugh.

"Yeah, I can't catch a break. I'm about to get up in a few minutes. I've been laying here all day."

"Yeah, do that because we gotta go grab some shit to wear for tonight. You know the club gonna be poppin' tonight!" said Psycho.

"Whatchu trying to do? Hit the mall up?"

"Yeah, I'm trying to hit Ross Park Mall. They just opened back up. You know that they were doing all that renovation over there. I wanna see what it's hittin' for. I heard that they got everything in that bitch, now. *True Religion* store, Nordstrom, *Louis V* and some more shit."

"Yeah, I heard they had a bunch of shit in there, too. Give me like 20 minutes and I'll meet you out front."

"Aight, bet."

Body got out of the bed and made his way to the bathroom. He brushed his teeth and took a quick shower. He grabbed a white t-shirt out of his drawer, a pair of dark denim jeans from off the floor and got dressed. He slipped on a pair of white on white low top air force ones and was out the door.

Arriving at the mall, Psycho and Body, both had pretty good ideas about what they were looking for. So, they headed straight to Nordstrom to pick up some accessories. Body purchased a pair of black *Gucci* hiking boots, a belt and a pair of Aviator frames.

Psycho wasn't interested in wearing *Gucci* for the night. So once Body was finished, they went to Saks, where he copped a pair of navy blue *Prada* sneakers and a pair of *Prada* frames. From there, they went to Macy's, where they both copped *Eurie Jabar* v-neck tees and a few pairs of their designer jeans. They used to favor *Rock & Republic* and *True Religion* jeans until the *Eurie Jabar Collection* came on the scene.

Once they were finished shopping the duo left the mall and headed back to the hood to handle their business. Later that night, they got dressed. They were prepared to go out and continue their birthday celebration. A celebration which had stretched out to a span of three-weeks.

Body wore a pair of black jeans with his black *Gucci* boots, a white v-neck t-shirt, and his *Gucci* frames. He complimented his outfit with a white-gold Cuban Link chain with a diamond encrusted cross pendant adorning his chest. There were also the diamond studs in his ears and the *Benny & Co.* watch with the black leather band and iced out bezel. Both, Psycho and Body, decided to treat themselves and splurged on some jewels at the beginning of the summer.

Psycho's list of jewels included a traditional gold Cuban Link chain with a diamond encrusted Jesus pendant. In his ears, were squared shaped diamond studs encased in a gold setting. His wrist sported a gold iced out *Presidential Rolex* that he robbed from some North Side nigga. His reasoning was that the nigga sold him some bad coke. The truth was, he liked the watch and the nigga in question was soft. So, in his mind, he *had* to have it.

Dressed and ready to roll, Body first put a padlock on his bedroom door to prevent Robin from coming home and searching through his things. She didn't normally steal from her children, but Body wasn't going to tempt her. He took all the necessary precautions to protect his valuables. After he was done locking up, he stepped outside to meet Psycho. He wouldn't have to worry about Jasmine tonight because she was staying at Mama Jones'. He and Psycho gave each other dap and embraced in a manly hug, before jumping into their respective whips.

Along with the splurge on new jewels for the summer, also, came a set of new vehicles. Both opted to purchase SUVs. All money getting niggas copped big trucks. They were easily able to, thanks to the steady flow of crack sales on Bentley Drive. Psycho bought himself a hunter green Ford Expedition. He laced it with a set of 23" rims, a state of the art sound system and a 13" TV monitor hanging from the ceiling of the truck, between the front and the rear seats. Body went for a black Lincoln Navigator. He had all the same features on his truck that Psycho had. The only difference was the style of rims selected, but they were both Jordans, 23 inches.

They decided on *Rock Jungle* for the night. It was always popping on the weekends and had a pretty decent capacity size. Rock Jungle held at least 1,500 people . Located on the Southside of Pittsburgh in Station Square, Rock Jungle Night Club was situated right next to downtown. It promised to be overflowing with all kinds of women.

Chapter 4

When Body and Psycho pulled up to the club, there was a long line of cars forming at the entrance of the parking lot. They pulled up and allowed the valet to park their trucks. They noticed the large crowds of people outside the club. They knew the spot would be *stupid* packed. Body and Psycho knew BJ, the club owner. So, they were able to gain immediate entrance through the side door and avoid the security and police checkpoints. They were able to walk into the club concealing two Glock .40's. As soon as they entered, they headed straight for the VIP section.

Once in the VIP, the first thing to catch their attention was a pair of bad ass Latinas. The girls were sitting at a table nursing their drinks when Body and Psycho approached them.

" Mind, if we join ya'll?" asked Body. The girls obliged.

"How you doing? I'm Body. This is my man, Psycho." Body said addressing the girls and shaking the hand of each.

"Nice to meet you. I'm Jennifer. This is my girl, Milagros." said the young lady.

Body sat down in front of Milagros. Psych was sitting in front of Jennifer. Both of the girls were beautiful, *but* Milagros was breathtaking. It was easy to see that she was aware of it from the air of sassiness she was exuding. She was a redbone, standing at 5' 7", which was tall for a girl. She stood towering over Psycho's 5'8" frame in her 4 inch *Christian Louboutin* open-toe stilettos. In her heels, she was nearly 6 feet tall, making her nearly eye level with Body. She had long, light brown hair with highlights of blonde throughout. The ends were neatly trimmed and the mane came to rest at the small of her back.

Body looked into her eyes and immediately noticed their greenish hazel color. He, also, noticed her pretty pink full lips that appeared to be covered in *Mac* lipgloss. *"Damn she's gorgeous"* , was the only thought Body could manage. She wore a pair of chandelier earrings, a red top that loosely dipped in the middle showing her ample cleavage and a pair of khaki short shorts that clung tightly to her firm thick legs and fat round ass. Body looked down and saw that she had some of the prettiest toes, he had ever seen. She had a French pedicure to match her manicure. Just the sight of her was making Body's dick hard.

Psycho was busy pushing up on Jennifer. She was fine, too. She was light-skinned and wore her jet-black hair in punk rock fashion. She wore gold doorknocker earrings and a white wife beater. Her C-cup breast, almost, bursting through the fabric. Her dark denim *Seven Jeans* fit her thick frame very tightly. On her feet were pink *Nine West* pumps.

"Where y'all from?" asked Body "I never seen y'all around here before."

"We're from Jersey." replied Jennifer. She was the most outspoken of the duo, "Bergen county." She said being more specific.

"We came here for school, but we don't hang out too much. Maybe, that's why you haven't seen us. Plus, we haven't been in town too long."

"Which school do y'all go to?" asked Psycho

"We go to the University of Pittsburgh."

"That's what's up. Y'all go to Pitt. Can we get y'all something to drink?"

"I'll take an Incredible Hulk." said Jennifer.

"And what about you, beautiful?" Body said referring to her friend, Milagros. He was trying to spark a conversation.

Her friend was willing to converse, but Body had yet to hear Milagros utter a word.

"I'm fine, thank you." said Milagros, finally responding to something.

Body detected the accent in her voice. He was certain she was Latina. He decided to use this as an opportunity to break the ice.

"Tu eres Hispana?" [1]

Milagros looked surprisingly at Body. "¡Claro que sí! Yo soy Boricua."[2] she replied.

"Me gusta las puertorriqueñas mucha."[3] said Body, after hearing her nationality.

"I like your name, what does it mean?" Asked Psycho, getting involved in the conversation.

"It means a surprise or miracle. My mom was under the impression that she was barren, until she got pregnant with me. My dad was also under that impression. So, I was quite the surprise for him and a miracle for my mom."

"That's dope." was all Body could say.

---

[1] Are you Hispanic?

[2] Of course, I am. I'm Boricua.

[3] I like Puerto Rican women a lot.

"You can call me *Mila*. Everyone close to me does." She smiled revealing a perfect set of white teeth.

The ice was broken. They spent the rest of the time getting to know each other. She was hands down the baddest bitch in the club, which made Body the envy of most *niggas* in the club that night. As the night came to an end, they said their goodbyes and exchanged contact info. Body and Psycho departed Rock Jungle and headed for Travelers.

Travelers was an after-hour spot located in the Homewood section on the borderline of East Liberty. Niggas whole reasoning for going to the Trav's was to scout out the stragglers. Psycho and Body struck gold when they ran into Temeeka and Marquesha. *They weren't in the club, but for a hot second before they were leaving with the girls.* They went straight to the Ramada Inn, where they purchased a room with double beds. They switched back and forth having pleasure with both girls.

Chapter 5

In the weeks that followed the birthday celebrations, Body and Mila were seeing a lot of each other. However, in the past few weeks, he had been grinding so hard in the streets. Mila hadn't seen or heard much of him. After pulling another late night shift, it wasn't until late afternoon when Body was awakened by the constant ringing of the phone. He checked the caller ID for missed calls. He noticed Psycho's number and remembered that he had some important things to discuss with him. He dialed Psych's number. Psycho answered after four rings.

"Yo!" he answered.

"What's popping, Ike? I got some things that I need to holla at you about. I need you to swing through." said Body.

"Aight, I'm in the crib. I'll be down there in like 3 minutes."

"Aight, bet." said Body.

Body hopped in the shower. By the time he was coming out of the bathroom, Jasmine was letting Psycho in. Psycho went into Body's room and sat down on the edge of the bed.

"So, what's good?" said Psycho.

"I've been doing a lot of thinking. We're doing aight right now on Bentley and we got the wholesale shit going, too. But, shit is getting hectic with these coke prices. Keys are steadily going up. We're paying $30k now, instead of $25k. *And from what I'm hearing,* that shit is gonna continue to rise. The drought is officially in effect. Dem bitches will be $40,000 in a minute!"

"So, what's the plan?" asked Psych.

"We gotta flex and adapt,my nigga. The plan is *dope*." said Body.

Chapter 6

Body's cell phone danced as it vibrated on the nightstand. An occurrence, he had long ago gotten accustomed with. He glanced at the clock. It was 6:12 pm. He had been sleeping all day due to all of the running he had been doing that week. He was slightly groggy, when he answered.

"Hello?"

"Hola Papi. ¿Cómo estás?"[4]

Body smiled, knowing exactly who was on the other end of the phone. Mila had been on his mind a lot, lately.

"Estoy bien Mami. ¿Cómo estas usted?"[5]

"¿Por qué no me llamaste?"[6] she asked, getting straight to the point.

"Porque, yo quisiera esperar.[7] I've just been a little busy, that's all. I didn't want to bother you with my mess." Body was switching from Spanish to English in the conversation. They often spoke in *Spanglish.*

"No es verdad Papi . No piensas como así."[8] she responded.

"Aight, you're right. But, what's good?" said Body.

---

[4] Hello Papi, how are you?

[5] I'm doing well, Mami. How are you?

[6] Why haven't you called me?

[7] Because I wanted to wait.

[8] That's not true, Papi. Don't think like that.

"Yo tengo mucho aburrido Papi."[9] said Mila.

"Oh is that the *only* reason you called me. Because you're *bored?*"

"Claro que no[10]. I wanna see you. I wanna take you out." said Mila.

"Oh, you gonna take *me* out?" asked Body, incredulously.

"Yup, what time do you want me to pick you up?" asked Mila.

He couldn't help, but laugh out loud. He had never had a girl pick him up and take *him* out. It was always the other way around. Most of the girls he knew, didn't even *have* a car to pick him up. Mila was becoming more intriguing to him. She had yet to cease impressing him.

"Aight. Well, where are you coming from?"

"I'm at home in Oakland." said Mila.

"Come through. I'm up Oak Hill." said Body.

"Oh, that's cool. Can you be ready by 8:00?"

"That's perfect."

When the call ended he immediately began looking for something to wear. He opted for a pair of denim jeans with faded crease lines in the upper thigh area by *Eurie Jabar Collection*. His choice of shirt was a white, long sleeve button up, also by *Eurie Jabar Collection*. He picked out a pair of black dress socks and a pair of low top black *Mauri* sneakers with the gator toe. To complete the outfit, he chose a black *Versace* blazer. Having his wardrobe intact for the night,

---

[9] I'm very bored right now, Papi.

[10] Of course not.

he took a quick shower. He sprayed on his *Lucky You* cologne and got dressed. Body looked himself over in the mirror and was happy with his vision. He put on his watch as a final touch. Five minutes later, his cell phone was ringing.

"Hello?"

"I'm coming into Oak Hill now. What's the address again?" asked Mila.

"228. You'll see the black Navigator in front." said Body.

"Alright, come outside."

Body padlocked his bedroom door and stepped outside. Mila was waiting outside in a brand new red Honda accord. Body got into the car and settled back into the tan leather seat. The interior of the car was very clean. This was the same way Body kept his own vehicle. It had a sweet smell from the peach air freshener that hung from the rearview mirror. Mila noticed the wardrobe that Body was wearing . She was impressed. She had never known a young man to dress so sharp. She was shocked when she discovered that Body was *only* 17 years old. He was intelligent, well beyond his years, mature, well spoken and respectful. It put him in a different class.

Mila took Body to a nice Italian restaurant on Carson Street, the Southside of Pittsburgh. In all his years of living in the city, he had never been to that spot. He found it ironic because he considered himself a "foodie". The restaurant was a quaint, little place. Body's imagination got the best of him. He began to wonder if Pittsburgh's Italian *mafia"* frequented the joint. Maybe, he was on to something or maybe he just watched too much *Sopranos.*

***

When Mila got out of the car she commanded all attention. Her black *Prada* dress hugged her curves. The waist flared out at the hips laying softly on her fat ass, almost as a tennis skirt would do. Her black open-toe, *Gucci* stilettos had pink soles. The shoe straps criss-crossed up her shaven legs and tied at the calves. She looked immaculate. Body was very impressed with her classiness.

They were seated and given menus to look over.

"This is a nice spot. I always drive past it and never considered going in." said Body.

"I'm glad you like it." said Mila.

"I'll judge how much I like it, after I taste the food." he responded.

The waitress came over interrupting their conversation, "Are you ready to order now or do you all need more time?"

"The lady will order first."

"I'll have the seafood lasagna, caesar salad, garlic bread and a bottle of Moscato, please."

"And for you, Sir?" asked the waitress.

"I'll have the seafood alfredo."

While they were waiting for their food to arrive, they continued to converse and learn more about each other. He learned that she had a pretty big family. Due mostly in part to her father, who bore children with many different women. She was of a mixed descent, a Puerto Rican mother and Columbian father. She was five years older than

Body at age 22. He opened up to her about his childhood, his drug addicted mother and the fact that he never met his father. Usually, he wouldn't tell people the things that he shared with her.

The food arrived. They ate and discussed their future plans.

"I like that you're going to school for business. I want to do some business myself, but I'm not sure what kind, yet. I just know that I would rather be an *employer* than an *employee*. I can't work for nobody. I'm not good at taking orders. I'd rather give them." said Body, overly confident. As he continued to speak, the intensity of Mila's gaze exposed her true feelings. *He was exactly what she'd been missing.*

"Sounds interesting and ambitious." said Mila.

"Another reason, I don't want to work for anyone is that I don't want to be extorted."

"Extorted? I don't understand." said Mila.

"Well, it's like this. When you work a job, you don't pay taxes. The government takes them from you. You never get to see that money. That's extortion, if I've ever seen it. Plus, when you work a job, you're paid a salary or hourly wage. No matter how hard you work, it doesn't affect your salary. Even, if the company does extremely well, the employees still make $10 to $12 an hour. You have to be on some corporate shit to win. It's different when you run your own shit. You get all kinds of options and perks that the regular 9-5 working man will never get." said Body.

"That's kind of deep, Jabar. It's very interesting. I never saw it like that before. You have a very unique way of seeing things."

After they finished their meal, Mila paid for dinner and they departed the restaurant. She drove across the Birmingham Bridge on her way back to the Hill. She reached Body's house and pulled over behind his Navigator. She got out of the car and walked him to the door. Once again, he was blown away and couldn't help, but smile. This girl was something else and he really liked her. She gave him a kiss goodnight and her full, soft lips mesmerized him.

"Hablar contigo más tarde Papi."[11]said Mila.

With that, she sashayed back to her car. Body was left standing there watching her. His dick was so hard, it began to cause him discomfort. She pulled away and he adjusted.

---

[11] Talk to you later, Papi.

Chapter 7

Body and Psycho were in Body's Navigator, driving down Baum Boulevard. They were smoking a blunt of haze while listening to the stereo system. Body had a Reggaeton song by RichyRicoTheGRP blaring through the speakers:

"Subete Subete, dale esta abajo suavecito suave.
Subete Subete, mami desnudate quitarte la ropas"

Psycho leaned forward and turned the volume down.

"Why you always listening to this *mira mira* shit, nigga?"

They immediately start laughing.

"Nigga, this *mira mira* shit helped me bag that bad ass chick in Rock Jungle, too." Body responded.

"Yea, you definitely got that shit off. You probably ain't even fuck that bitch, yet."

He sat there quietly without responding. Psycho looked over at him in disbelief.

"Yo, not my nigga! You still ain't hit that?"

Laughter filled the truck.

Psycho thought that was hilarious. He was bending over with laughter, "You slippin' nigga."

"Aight, nigga. It ain't *that* funny."

"Shit nigga, we met them bitches months ago. I would've been left her ass alone, if she was on that shit with me. What's good with that?" Psycho asked.

"She wanna settle down, my nigga. She ain't with none of that other shit. I haven't been acting all pressed, either. I'm out here getting different bitches every night and it ain't like I'm spending no money on her. Shit, the last time we went out she paid for everything."

"That's what's up. But, whatchu gonna do? You gonna settle down?" asked Psycho.

"I might." said Body.

Psycho began to laugh again, "Sucker for love umm umm sucker for love."

"Fuck you, nigga." Body said playfully. "Keep laughing, nigga. But, I'm making shit slap. Remember, when I was telling you about making the switch and fucking with the dope game?" asked Body.

"Hell yeah, I remember and we need to be making something slap soon. Keys of the yay are at $35,000 and rising quick. I've been hollering at a few niggas. I can get rid of some bricks, if we can get our hands on something official." said Psycho.

"That's what it is. We should definitely be able to get our hands on something official, shortly. While you over there laughing and shit, ol' girl is plugging me in nigga." said Body.

"Plugging you in?" asked Psycho with a confused look on his face.

"Yup. It turns out that her dad is Colombian and that nigga is *heavy* in the dope game. She got a brother in New Jersey, who be moving shit here in the states. They got different Moms and shit, but the same dad. He's full-blooded Colombian, some nigga named Carlito. I already hollered at him. Me and Mila going up to meet him in person tomorrow, so we can discuss everything in detail. He don't play the phones real heavy either, so that was a good sign. How you like that for sucker for love, nigga?"

It was Body's turn to laugh now.

"That's what it is. How much the bricks goin' for?" asked Psycho.

"I haven't decided yet. I was thinking somewhere between $225 to $250." said Body.

"Nah, I mean how much we paying per brick?" asked Psycho.

"We ain't buying no bricks, Ike. This nigga got that raw dope. It's supposed to be that *deal.* So, we're gonna make our own bricks. It'll be more prosperous for us that way." said Body.

"Yeah, that shit sounds all good. But, I don't know shit about cooking no dope." said Psycho. "My thing has always been the coke game, but a nigga can flex and adapt."

Body enjoyed another good laugh at Psycho's expense.

"You don't have to cook no dope, my nigga. We just gotta cut it to prevent motherfuckers from overdosing." said Body.

"I don't know how to do that shit either." Psycho replied.

"Don't worry about all that. I don't know how to cut that shit myself, but I have all of that covered. One thing for certain, two things for sure. I can sell that shit. It's like this, my raise has been a dope fiend longer than I've been alive. Besides giving me life, she ain't never done a damn thing for me. Given her condition, she's never been able to. But, now she can. She's gonna cut the dope for us and make sure that shit comes back official. She's gonna sample that shit, too. Fuck it. She ain't gonna stop getting high, until she's ready. She's 40 years old now, dawg. I don't want to give her no dope. But, if I don't she's just gonna steal that shit. It is what it is." said Body.

"You sure about this, Ike?" asked Psycho. He was wearing a look of concern on his face.

"Yeah, I'm sure. I already spoke to her about it. *And* of course, she ain't turning down no free high. Before, I was only selling crack, but that wasn't her drug of choice. So, I would just give her money, *knowing* what she was gonna do with it. I always knew she was spending the money I gave her to get high. She sure wasn't spending it on groceries. I just didn't want her running around in the streets like a zombie or sucking dicks to support her habit."

"I feel you, my nigga." said Psycho.

"Aight look, me and Mila gotta get a rental. We need to get that shit tonight, so we can split in the a.m. I'm gonna shoot to Jersey real quick. As soon as I get back, I'll let you know what's good with the numbers and shit."

***

Body called Mila to ensure that she made the reservations for the car rental. She answered after two rings.

"Hello." answered Mila.

"What's up, Mami?"

"Nada Papi. Esperando para ti.[12] What's good?"

"Did you make the reservations for the rental?"

"Yup, I got a '07 Ford Explorer." said Mila.

"That's cool. Can we pick it up, tonight?" asked Body.

"I guess so. Is everything alright?"

"Yeah, everything is cool. I just want to leave first thing in the morning. So, I wanted to get the rental now and you can stay the night with me. I figured, we can bounce early." said Body.

Mila smiled to herself.

"I bet you did figure that." she said playfully.

"It ain't even like that. So, stop tripping." he replied.

"We'll see. Aight, let's go get the car. Can you come get me?" asked Mila.

"Where you at?"

"I'm in Squirrel Hill at Jennifer's."

"I know where that is. But, check this. Drive home. Drop off your car and I'll pick you up from there." said Body.

"Ok, Papi." said Mila.

Body ended his call and addressed Psych.

"Yo, I'm about to shoot to Oakland, real quick. I need to pick up Mila, so she can take me to grab the rental."

"Aight." responded Psych.

Getting close to East Liberty, Body made a U-turn and headed to Mila's place. She was parked in front waiting for him to arrive. When

---

[12] Nothing, Papi. Waiting for you.

she saw the Navigator pull up, she got out of her car and hit the automatic lock. Then, she got in the truck with Body and Psycho.

"Where did you reserve the car at, Mami?" asked Body.

"The airport." said Mila.

Body jumped on the Parkway and headed toward the airport. It was nearly a half hour later when they arrived. Mila and Body got out of the truck and went inside to pick up the rental, leaving Psycho to wait in the car. Fifteen minutes later, they emerged from the lot in a gray Ford Explorer. Body gave Psycho a quick head nod and Psycho drove off. Getting comfortable in the rental, Body popped in Jay-Z's "American Gangster" CD before hitting the parkway toward downtown.

Thirty minutes later, Body and Mila pulled into the Westin Hotel. The valet approached the driver side. He handed Body a ticket stub and then proceeded to park the SUV. Body went to the front desk to see what kind of rooms were available. This was one of the most prestigious hotels in Pittsburgh and they were often sold out. Under those circumstances, you would be directed to their sister hotel, the Sheraton in Station Square. On this particular night, however, Body was in luck. There was a room available on the 16th floor.

Body and Mila boarded the elevator and got off on the 16th floor in search of 1621. The room was nice. It was equipped with a small sitting area, a couch, coffee table and an entertainment center with a 32" TV. There were, also, two remote controls for a Nintendo 64. The first thing that grabbed his attention was the hot tub. He was already making plans in his mind. As luck would have it, the hot tub was the first thing to grab Mila's attention, as well.

Body kicked off his shoes, plopped down on the bed and grabbed the remote. He flicked through the channels until he found what he was looking for, the menu that allowed him to select music. He saw the classic album by Jodeci and immediately went to their hit single, *Feenin'*. He knew that would be the album he selected for the night. He started the music and let it play softly through the speakers of the TV.

K-Ci sang:

"Take my money, my house and my cars. For one hit of you, you can have it all, Baby Baby. 'Cause makin' love, everytime we do girl, It's worse than drugs cause, I'm an addict of you. I can't leave you alone. You got me feenin'... feenin'.... feenin'"

Body picked up the phone to order room service. He ordered a bottle of *Moet* and a platter of fresh strawberries. When he hung up the phone, Mila was coming out of the bathroom wrapped in a towel. He looked at her beautiful face. It was moist from the dew of the shower. Her ever flowing, thick mane of hair was damp, causing it to stick to her shoulders. Her firm calves and thick thighs still held pellets of water on them. Body imagined they could quench his thirst.

Mila noticed him staring and couldn't help from smiling.

"What you looking at, nigga?"

He looked her up and down from head to toe. Then, looked into her eyes before he replied, "Ya fine ass."

Mila blushed. She had a rosy red hue in her cheeks. Their moment was interrupted by a knock on the door. Mila was surprised that someone would be knocking. Body reassured her that everything was fine.

"That's just room service."

"You ordered?"

Body smiled, "Why wouldn't I?"

He opened the door and took the champagne and strawberry platter. Body handed the lady a twenty dollar tip for her quick service. He shut the door and set the platter on the nightstand. Then, he went over to warm up the hot tub.

"I hope you brought a bathing suit." said Mila. "Lucky for you, I'm comfortable in my birthday suit."

She dropped her towel to the floor exposing the nakedness of her body. Body lustfully looked at her beautiful C-cup breast with large areolas and pink nipples. Her breasts were firm. Her nipples stood erect due to the moistness of her body and the slight breeze that made its way into the room. Body let his eyes roam over her nude body. He looked at her firm, flat abs. Her navel was adorned with an iced out butterfly. His eyes continued downward looking at her wide hips and the peek-a-boo sight of her pink pussy. It was neatly shaved into a landing strip pattern.

Mila stood still a moment, giving Body an opportunity to take it all in. She then strutted over to the hot tub. Body watched as her hips swayed from side to side. Her fat round ass looked perfect as it gave a slight jiggle. At the hot tub, Mila stuck her left foot into the water to test the temperature. Seeing that the water was warm, she stepped into the hot tub and sat down facing him.

"You shy?" She was taunting him.

"Not at all." was his reply.

He took off his socks first. Then, he unfastened his jeans letting them drop to the floor. Next, he started to take off his v-neck t-shirt. Starting from the bottom and flexing his abs to give Mila a view of his ripped midsection. He threw the t-shirt in the corner. He was now standing in the middle of the floor in nothing, but his *Eurie Jabar* boxer briefs. Mila lustfully watched him in anticipation. He pulled his boxer briefs down and stood before her with a semi-hard dick dangling between his legs. Mila's mouth watered, slightly. She was surprised by the size of it and it showed in her school-girl blush. She sat in the hot tub and stared at Body's manhood trying to estimate the size. Her guesstimation caused her clit to throb and pussy to moisten in excitement.

Body walked over to the nightstand to retrieve the champagne bucket and the strawberry platter. He grabbed the blunt of sour diesel, put the platter down next to the hot tub and stepped in. Not caring to use the champagne flutes, he swigged from the bottle. He passed the blunt to Mila and she pulled on it a few times. The weed was so strong that Mila was sky high, after three hits of the blunt. He passed her the bottle of Moet as she passed back the blunt. The bottle was nearly a quarter of the way gone.

Mila stood up in front of Body. Pulling on the blunt, he looked up at her. She reached past him and grabbed the ice bucket.

"The champagne's not chilled enough for you?"

"The champagne is fine. The ice is for you."

She had him sit on the edge of the hot tub. She popped a couple of pieces of ice into her mouth and got on her knees She then grabbed his dick in her small hands and stuffed it in her ice-filled mouth. His dick responded immediately, becoming rock hard and standing at full attention. Mila worked the muscles of her mouth and esophagus as she deepthroats his dick and massaged his balls with her free hand. This was driving him crazy. He wasn't sure of how much more he could take, as his toes began to curl. Mila was slurping Body's dick and licking it up and down. She went down and started to suck his balls and stroke his dick, simultaneously.

She moaned softly, "I wanna taste you, Papi."

Those were the only words Body needed to hear. As Mila began sucking his dick again, the head of Body's dick mushroomed and erupted in Mila's mouth. She wasn't shy. She swallowed every drop. Body sat Mila on the end of the hot tub and picked up the bottle of Moet. He poured it all over her starting at the collarbone. Licking it from her clavicle, sucking it from her titties and slurping it from her navel. He grabbed the underside of her knees and pushed her legs back. He buried his face in her pussy, licking up all of her juices. He sucked on her clit and felt it swell in his mouth. Simultaneously, he sucked her clit and rapidly licked it back & forth causing her body to go into convulsions.

He took a strawberry from the platter and thrust it into her pussy. She grabbed him with both hands by the back of his head, moaned loudly and came in his mouth. He picked Mila up and carried her to the bed. She watched intently, as he ate the strawberry that was once buried in her love tunnel. She laid back on the bed and put her legs on Body's muscular shoulders. He pulled her closer to the edge of the bed and slowly eased his dick inside her warm tight pussy. She moaned and arched her back. The tight squeeze made her believe that she may have underestimated him.

He took her feet from his shoulders and began sucking her toes, grinding deep inside her and massaging her clit at the same time. Mila came twice, before Body flipped her over and began fucking her hard from the back and spanking her ass. They made love throughout the night and fell asleep in each other's arms.

Chapter 8

The plan was to wake up bright and early and hit the road by at least 6:00 a.m. The long night of lovemaking made it hard to make the deadline. The ringing of the phone had awakened both Body and Mila.

"Hello?"

"It's checkout time, Sir." replied the hotel staff.

Body looked over at the digital clock on the nightstand. It read 11:05 a.m.

"Shit! Alright, thank you."

He hung up the phone. "Come on, Baby. We gotta get moving."

Body and Mila showered together. They dressed and were out the door. The valet brought the Explorer to the entrance of the hotel. Body tipped the valet and got into the driver's seat. The couple hit the highway en route to Elizabeth, New Jersey.

The long road trip left the couple plenty of time to talk about the previous night, as well as the future. They both expressed how they felt about the other. By the end of the trip, their relationship was established.

It took 7 hours to arrive in New Jersey, including the stops for food and gas. When they arrived in Elizabeth, Carlito was waiting for them at a BP gas station right off exit 13A on the New Jersey

Turnpike. He was driving a black, shiny Range Rover. Body followed the Range, until they came to an apartment building on Marshall Street in the downtown section of the city. Carlito got out of his truck, while Body and Mila exited the Explorer. Mila embraced Carlito.

"¿Qué pasa Papi? ¡Te extraño!"[13]

"¡Te extraño también! ¿Cómo estás?"[14]

"Estoy bien."[15]

"You look good, girl. You're getting all grown on me." Carlito smiled.

Mila smiled back and said, "Lito, this is my boyfriend, Body."

Body and Carlito shook hands.

"Nice to meet you." said Lito with a headnod.

"Likewise." responded Body.

"My sister tells me you're a good guy. She's *never* vouched for anyone before. Come, I wanna show you something." said Lito.

They all walked up the stairs to the third floor and entered a small apartment. There was no furniture in the living room, just a few *Office Depot* tables and chairs. There were eight people in the room in total. Each of them taping and folding stamped bags of dope. In one of the two bedrooms, were three more tables and six more people bagging up dope. Carlito explained how the operation ran to Body, so he would have a good understanding.

---

[13] What's up, Papi? I missed you!

[14] I miss you too! How are you?

[15] I'm doing good.

"I have quite a few setups like this. I put this together to make sure my team eats, too. I usually don't come here. I deal with the weight side of the business. I know you're new to the dope game, so I'm giving you a little game. After all, the better you do, the better I do."

"No doubt." said Body.

"De Nada.[16] Come with me. We have many things to discuss. Mila, I'm gonna take you to see Abuela. Me and Body have things to take care of."

"Okay." said Mila.

The three of them left the apartment.

"As a matter of fact, Body will ride with me and you take *that* truck."

Body passed her the keys. He gave her a kiss and then climbed into the Range with Lito. Mila got in the Explorer. She adjusted the seat and headed to her grandma's house on Cross Ave.

Carlito and Body spent the next few hours getting to know each other and discussing the Pittsburgh market. Later that night, Carlito took Body to a popular strip club called *Jersey Girls*. He knew the men at the door, so he and Body were able bypass the long line. As per usual, it was a packed Friday night. The men had a table in the VIP section, where Carlito ordered bottles of *Moet*, *Ace of Spades* and *Hennessy*. Body was his guest, so the festivities were on Lito. He went to the cashier window and exchanged for $10,000 worth of singles. He gave $5,000 of the singles to Body. The men laughed, joked and threw

---

[16] You're welcome.

wads of cash at the dancers. In the middle of lap dances, Carlito leaned over, so Body could hear him speak.

"I'll give you the birds for $60,000. It's pure. You can put 1,000 grams on each bird and sell it wholesale. It'll still be much better than anything out here." Carlito yelled over the music.

Albeit, he was new to the dope game. Body was well aware that *the money was in the cut*. The bigger cut you could use for the product, the bigger the profit. Body listened intently as Carlito spoke.

"I'll give you one kilo to take with you. You can pay me when you finish. Esta bien?"[17]

Body nodded his head in affirmation.

The men enjoyed the rest of the night with the Brazilian strippers. After a few hours, they departed the club.

✳✳✳

It was late when Carlito pulled in front of his grandma's house on Cross Avenue in Midtown. Carlito called Mila and told her to have the door open for Body.

"Aight, I'll bring the work here before you leave." said Carlito.

"I wanna get on the road around 5 am." said Body.

Carlito looked at his watch, "It's almost 4 am now. I'll be back shortly."

"Aight." said Body. He gave Carlito dap and got out the SUV.

---

[17] Okay?

Mila opened the door, tiredly. Body entered the house, closed the door and secured the deadbolt out of habit. Mila laid back down on the couch and went back to sleep.

Forty-five minutes later, Carlito entered the house. He put down a box on the floor that he was carrying. He wore a small duffle attached to a strap, slung across his shoulder. He unzipped the bag and passed Body a package in the shape of a shoe.

"That's how we do it. Each shoe is a half a key. There's another one in the bag."

Body examined the shoe that was tightly wrapped and covered with carbon paper and black tape. Carlito tossed him the bag.

"That's everything you'll need to get started. I chose a name for it, already. But we can easily change it, if you don't like it."

Body looked inside the box, first. It contained smaller boxes of glassine bags, a stamp that read *Obsession*, and blocks of benita to cut the dope.

"This name is cool, right here."

"Aight, I gotta get going. Mila knows the ropes. She'll show you what's up."

Carlito gave Mila a hug, Body a pound and was on his way out the door.

"Wait, where's the spray?" asked Mila concernedly.

"It's in the bag, too." responded Carlito.

"Aight." said Mila.

Carlito closed the door behind him and was gone. Mila checked the bag and found what she was looking for.

"What's the spray for?" asked Body.

"It's to keep dogs away, in case we get pulled over or something. We spray the outside of the bag and all around the car or anywhere we put the work. It works wonders and will keep us out of jail."

"How do you know so much about this?" asked Body.

"I'm Zeus' daughter. She said with a shrug of the shoulders. Plus, I used to transport for my brother sometimes, when he was first getting started. I even used to help run the bag up spot. So, I know a thing or two about the game."

"I knew there was a reason I liked you." Body said with a smile.

"Aight, let's get going. I'll drive and you can get some rest," said Mila.

She grabbed the keys and the small travel bag containing the dope and paraphernalia. Mila headed out the door. She opened the back hatch to the truck and began to spray the interior. She lifted the panel where the spare tire was kept and sprayed in there as well. Then, she placed the bag inside and closed it back. Next, she closed the hatch and sprayed the outside, too. She took the empty can back into the house and threw it away. After she finished, they were ready to hit the road. Body was in the passenger seat waiting for her. She started the engine, put on her Alicia Keys album and headed west towards Pittsburgh.

Body was awoken by Mila shaking his shoulder and calling his name.

"Jabar! We're home." She was the only woman outside his raise or his little sister who could call him by his birth name. He just wasn't interested in getting that acquainted with too many people.

He opened his eyes and noticed that he was at Mila's place in Oakland. He was so tired from the night before that he slept through the entire drive home. He and Mila exited the car, retrieved the bag and they went inside.

Body made love to Mila as soon as they closed the door. He had been waiting for a chance to get her by herself. Seeing this ride-or-die side of her brought out the animalistic nature in him. It was difficult to keep his hands off of her. After fucking up a sweat for the next hour, he was ready to get down to business. He picked up his cell phone and dialed Psycho.

"Yo! What's the drill?" answered Psycho.

"I'm back."

"Where you at?"

"I'm at my girl's crib."

"Ya girl's crib? Oh you got a girl, now? Not my boy." Psycho laughed.

"Whatever, nigga. Just get over here, so we can get to business." Body replied.

"I'll be there in like 10 minutes. I'm on Bentley."

"Aight, bet." replied Body.

Being on *"Black People time"*, it was a half hour later when Psycho arrived.

"What's good, Bro? What happened up there?"

"This is what happened." said Body.

He pulled out the small travel bag and placed it on the kitchen countertop. He removed the two shoes and dropped them on the counter with a thud.

"What's that?" asked Psych. A slight smirk was etched on his face, anticipating the answer.

"That's a bird. Each one is a half. They walk them shits in the country everyday from Mexico. All the factory workers that have to cross through the border. They each bring a bird with them in their shoes. Border Patrol are looking for big shipments, so 300 to 500 workers can easily slip through with 300 to 500 birds a day. We owe $30,000 a pop for this shit. We pay $60,000 per bird."

"Damn, that's good as hell."

"Hell yeah, my nigga. Let's get paid."

***

Body and Psych bought chairs and tables from *Office Depot* like the one's Body saw at Carlito's spot. They also bought a tape dispenser, dozens of bags of small black rubber bands and a coffee grinder. They used the spare bedroom in Mila's condo to set up shop, initially. Body sent Mila to Oakhill to pick up Robin. Twenty minutes later the ladies arrived.

"Hey, mom." said Body.

"Hey, Baby." said Robin as she hugged Body.

Everyone could sense her excitement and anxiousness.

"Hi, Miss Robin." said Psych.

He was respectful to Robin. She may have been an addict, but she was also his best friend's raise.

"Hey, Baby." said Robin.

She hugged him as well.

"Aight, let's get started." said Body.

They all went upstairs to the workroom, where Body cut open the shoe for Robin to examine. A strong vinegar-like odor wafted through the room.

"Damn, that's some strong shit. What do you have to cut it with?" asked Robin.

"I just got this benita that the connect gave me." replied Body.

"Well, that will have to do for now. But, there are much better things to use. We need some fentanyl, but it's kinda hard to get. I know where to get some powder-based morphine, though. Give me that benita for now."

Robin opened the benita. She broke it down on a plate and placed it in the microwave.

"Why you putting that in the microwave, mom?"

"Benita is just sugar, baby. You have to cook away the sweetness."

She blended the dope with the cut. Robin took a small portion to the bathroom and didn't return for 35 minutes. Starting to worry, Body knocked on the bathroom door.

Robin emerged looking sky high and said, "You got ya self a winner, baby. I ain't never had nothing like that."

All he could do was smile.

Body and Mila sat at one of the cheap *Office Depot* tables with a mound of dope in front of them. They would put the dope in the bags. Then, pass them to Robin and Psycho at the other table for taping and folding. The next step was to bundle the bags in tens. They did this for the entire day. They took breaks only to eat or use the bathroom. Body went to the drug store earlier and purchased face masks for everyone to wear and a bottle of *No Doz*.

"What are the pills for?" asked Psycho.

"They're caffeine pills to help you stay awake. We need to get this shit done." said Body.

He knew that it would take them a few days at least to put all the bricks together. *He, also, knew it would be his last time at the table.* He would put a team together how Carlito had. The dope was stronger than he had imagined. Robin had to put at least three gram of cut for every gram of dope to prevent killing herself. Even with a three on one, the dope was much stronger than anything Robin had ever seen. Starting with 1,000 grams, Body ended up with 4,000 grams of Grade-A heroin. He and Psych went out to holla at a few people and gave out samples. Before they could make it back home, their phones were ringing off the hook with orders. Some wanted 100 bricks. Some wanted 250 bricks and one person wanted 500. They were also receiving orders for raw material. They were excited to say the least.

"Damn. We 'bout to get rich! How much we got ready?"

"About 600, last I checked." said Psych.

"Aight, cool. That last call was from the nigga who owned the club in Station Square."

"What he say?" asked Psych.

"He wants 1,500 of them shits."

"1,500? How much did you tell him?"

"I told him $150. We need to get rid of this shit. The longer we hold it, the more chances we have to get caught with it. This shit is out of here. That's $225,000 and we can get at least another 1,000 bricks out that shit. I ain't never seen no dope like this! Niggas would kill for this connect."

***

In three days, Body and Psycho managed to sell all the dope. They elected not to bag it all up. Instead, they sold the majority of it in weight. It was less of a headache. There was a big demand in the city of Pittsburgh for good dope. With dope like this, they were sure to corner the market. Body devised a plan. He would make one more trip to New Jersey as a show of good faith. Then, he would only send Mila to speak with Carlito. He would have runners to do the picking up. He figured that Carlito wouldn't snitch on his sister, so he preferred to have her speak on his behalf.

Having rented the Explorer for a week and only having it for 4 days, Body would use it to go back to New Jersey. He wasn't too worried about using it again because he wasn't picking up. He grabbed the same travel bag that Carlito gave him and stuffed it with $360,000. $60,000 was the money that Body owed Carlito and $300,000 was for an additional five birds.

Carlito was very pleased with Body's progress and swift execution. Carlito assured Body the five birds he paid for would be delivered with an additional five on consignment. When Body and Mila got close to Pittsburgh, he called Psycho on his cell phone.

"Yo." Answered Psych.

"Yo, I'm almost there. Meet me at the crib. One."

Body had already made his necessary detour to claim the package that awaited him. Twenty minutes later, they were pulling up at Mila's place where Psych was parked outside in his Expedition. Everyone exited their vehicles and entered the condo.

Body got right down to business. He threw the duffle bag on the kitchen counter and began pulling out shoes. Psycho watched in amazement as shoe after shoe was placed on the counter. There were ten pairs in total.

"Damn, what the fuck we gonna do with all this shit?" asked Psych.

"Nigga, we gonna sell it! But, first thing first. We're dealing on a completely different level now and we have to take more precautions. The first thing we gotta do is get new phones. We ain't fucking with the coke for right now, so we don't need these phones. Plus, everybody got these numbers, which is a good way to get indicted. We need a business phone and a leisure phone." said Body.

"That's smart," said Psych, nodding his head in agreeance.

"The business phones will be prepaid, so they don't have to be in anyone's name. We'll change up phones every other week. The most important thing is to make sure you never talk business on the phone. We have cars, so we can go meet niggas. The last thing we want is to end up on somebody's wiretap. Speaking of the cars, we need business cars, too. As soon as we start to recuperate on this flip, we can hit Route 51 and cop some used shit. I talked to Carlito when I was in Jersey and he said he can get us hooked up with some stash boxes."

"Aight, all that shit is official. But, what are we gonna do with all this dope? We already know how strong this shit is. Once we cut it, we're gonna have 40,000 grams of this shit." said Psycho.

"Not exactly. We're gonna get into the wholesale game even more. I know some niggas that will buy this shit by the birds. I've been talking to this crip nigga from Duquesne named D-Loc. He wants some birds. I told him $90,000 a pop. Everything should run smoothly. We leave enough room on the dope for other niggas to cut it and we move this shit a lot faster." said Body.

Psych just smiled as he was calculating the numbers in his head.

"So, what do you think?" asked Body.

"You're a genius, Ike. But...I think we gonna need some more guns!"

Chapter 9

Body and Psycho were working overtime to get the word out about their product. The plan was to serve someone from each part of the city. They knew that no one could compete with their product. So, if they had at least one person in each area, that's all it would take to conquer most of the city's clientele. In the city of Pittsburgh, the game was more or less a free-for-all. As long as you were from the area, you could set up shop. There was no organization. It was every man for himself. This was a weakness that Body noticed and an opportunity that he wanted to exploit. Having such a large supply of dope, Body was considering opening up blocks to move his product on a consistent basis. At the end of the day, he needed to impress the plug. He rode around in a rented Nissan Maxima and shared his thoughts with Psycho.

"Man, I've been thinking. We should open up our own blocks." said Body.

"Honestly, I've been thinking the same shit. Why you think I said we're gonna need some more guns?"

"I figured as much. That shit is gonna be easy for us to do. Look at how we took over on Bentley. We didn't even have to use any muscle 'cause them niggas already *knew* our reputation and how we get down. All we had to do was have good crack and slightly bigger rocks. Can't be much different with this dope. We put out the best shit and we got the spot. If niggas flex, we handle that shit, appropriately." said Body.

"See, that's why you my nigga, Ike. You be on point. Truth be told, I'm bored and I hope niggas flex. I need some rec. Where do we start though? 'Cause we can't sell dope on Bentley. There's no market for it." said Psych'.

"Nah, but we can sell it on Centre." responded Body.

Being from the Hill District, it was only natural for Body and Psycho to decide to start at home. However, there were two problems facing the men. The first was that all of the projects on the Hill contained money-making potential from crack sells. No set of projects on the Hill sold dope. However, there was Centre Avenue. Before the riots, Centre was once a prestigious area in the Black community. Something was always happening on Centre in its heyday. It was home to many businesses, including movie theaters, laundromats, bars, clubs, diners, salons, etc. Somehow, it turned into the place to go for your next fix.

The Hill District was dubbed as "Little New York" due to its projects being the city's Crack Capitol and the fast pace of it's lifestyle. It has since slowed down. Yet, a lot of money passed through Centre. Body and Psycho believed that they could bring Centre back to its heyday. Attempting to accomplish such a feat, however, would create problem number two for them. They couldn't make a move for Centre without conflict and potentially starting a war with Marvin.

Though the Hill District was every man for himself in the game, Centre was slightly different. Marv' supplied all the dope that was distributed on Centre. He had no true claim to it, but he wouldn't look kindly upon someone cutting in on his money. He had been in the game longer than Body and Psych had been alive. Marv' was an old-head. At forty-five years old, he had been in the dope game for over twenty five years. He was a *bonafide millionaire* with an assortment of legitimate businesses throughout the city. His businesses included, barbershops, car washes, convenience stores, bars, and nightclubs.

Back in the day, Marv' came up through the ranks the same way any young hustler would, if he planned to take over a dope spot that was a certified goldmine. He came up playing the murder game. Marv' played the murder game a little different than the normal gunslinger. In fact, he wasn't a gunslinger at all. Marv' was only a businessman. He would pay someone else to do his dirty work. Marv' never had to bust a gun in his life. His cousin 2-Gunz, or "Gunz" as he was sometimes referred to, had no problem busting guns for him. Gunz was also an old head. He and Marv' grew up together in R.C. projects. Gunz was four years younger than Marv'. Growing up, he quickly earned a reputation as *being crazy.*

Back then, R.C. was the home to most of the city's ballers. They all got their start in R.C. Gunz was no different, except that he didn't earn his money. He took it. He would rob the hustlers late night, after they were done hustling. One on one, in pairs or small groups, he would catch the hustlers lingering in one of the project courts. He preferred to catch them out of the view of onlookers. The last thing he needed was a witness. He would rather force them into a secluded hallway and then take *everything* they had.

Niggas were scared of Gunz because he was such a ruthless stickup kid. He was known to catch niggas slipping in the middle of the winter and take their coats and boots. He would force them into the hallway and make them strip. He knew the game well and was anticipating that most niggas kept crack in their asses. He would perform a search as thorough as any prison guard.

One night, in particular, Gunz caught three niggas slipping standing in front of a hallway smoking a blunt and bullshitting around. It just so happens, he was well equipped to run down on the group of men with a pistol grip riot pump shotgun. He slowly crept up on the trio, careful not to be seen until he was close enough, so that no one would run or pull out a gun. Oblivious to what was going on around them, they continued to smoke and joke. Once Gunz was close enough, he pulled the shotgun hidden beneath his trench coat and cocked it into action.

"Don't fucking move nigga! You know the rules!" said Gunz.

"Fuck!" one of the men exclaimed. Knowing he had an ounce of crack and a few thousand dollars in his pocket.

"Everybody get in the fucking hallway! Everybody face the wall and put your hands behind your head. Lock ya fingers!" screamed Gunz.

One by one, the men filed into the hallway and did as they were told.

"Now, down on your knees and cross ya legs at the ankles. One over the other." demanded Gunz.

He employed the same tactics as the police to secure his victims.

As the men obliged, he began his well-rehearsed routine. He would have one man stand at a time. He would instruct the man to take off his coat and shirt first to make sure there were no guns. Then, it was the shoes and socks, all the while facing the wall under the imminent threat posed by the barrel of the shotgun. The next step was the pants. Depending on the mood he was in, it could be the underwear, too. Gunz would toss a large travel bag and make them put everything inside. He would make them drop his drawers, squat and cough. This was a humiliating experience for the men. But nevertheless, they did as they were told. No one dared to defy him. One at a time, each man was faced with the same humiliation. Each packed their leather Avirex jackets and clothes into the bag, as well as any crack that fell from their asses, during the squat and cough procedures. Then, Gunz would disappear like a thief in the night.

He developed his routine because it was faster and safer. He didn't have time to pat-down niggas for weapons and look for places they may have stashed the money or drugs. He was well aware that niggas would cut holes in the lining of their coats as stash spots. So, he just took everything. Later, he could be seen wearing it. Gunz just didn't give a fuck. On the days that the new Jordan's came out, he would go straight to the hood, already knowing who wore his size. Either they would buy him some or he would take theirs. He started in R.C. and then stretched out across the Hill District. Eventually, he would do the same to niggas from all over the city. No one was exempt from 2-Gunz's wrath, not even the bitches.

If he saw a girl with a nice leather, a *Coach* bag, or anything that was hot at the time, he would rob her and give the items to his girl or whatever bitch he was trying to fuck at the moment. If he pushed up on some girls and felt like they were playing him, they got robbed, too. Gunz was just like that, a loose cannon.

His older cousin Marvin was an opportunist. He even found opportunity in the irrational behavior of Gunz. Although he wasn't the one pulling the trigger, Marv' was still ruthless. He was cunning like a fox and he was not to be trusted. Marv' started off selling crack in R.C. Eventually, he graduated to supplying weight to all the hustlers who posted up there daily. Once he was introduced to the dope game, he began hustling on Centre Ave. He saw potential to make more money by expanding his operation. The problem was that there were niggas on Centre, before Marv', who had most of the avenue locked down. He came up with a plan. He enlisted the help of his little cousin, Gunz. From that day forward, Gunz was to stop robbing niggas and *especially* bitches. He would now work strictly for Marv' and be well taken care of. The first plan of action was to eliminate the competition. The competition was Biggs.

Biggs was what you would call a *throwback* hustler. He had most of Centre Ave locked down, selling balloons of dope and speedballs. Those were the balloons which contained both dope *and* crack. Back in those days, it was Biggs who was the main supplier. Correction. He was the *only* supplier for the entire stretch of the avenue. Marv' accredited Biggs success to happenstance. But, if he had anything to say about it, all that would soon change. Being known for having a knack for hustling, it was relatively easy for Marv' to cut into Biggs.

He had a sit down with Biggs and his right-hand man, Trigger. Marv' told Biggs about his ambitions concerning the dope game and needing a supply. He told Biggs how he had a few outlets for dope in large quantities, which was true. He asked Biggs permission to pump on Centre, as well. Biggs liked the spirit of the young hustler. But, Trigger was leary. At the end of the day, it was Biggs' call and Biggs wanted the money that Marv' could bring in.

Marv' told Biggs that he needed dope in abundance. He would need a kilo. He told Biggs that he had the money to pay for half up front. Back then, a kilo of heroin was going for the upwards of $120,000. Biggs was impressed that the youngster could come up with $60,000 up front. Biggs obliged and fronted the other half to Marv' on consignment.

Marv' met up with Biggs and Trigg in a vacant lot of a strip mall off of Frankstown Road. This would serve as their meeting spot. This specific place was chosen because it was out of view and had close proximity to different areas on the East Side of Pittsburgh. Marv' would follow the same routine every time he met with Biggs and Trigg. He would exit his car, make small talk and lead the men around the back of the car to retrieve the money from the trunk.

He would exchange the money for the drugs. He paid Biggs the money he owed for the consignment and an additional $60,000 to purchase another half of key. After a few short trips, the plan changed. But, the routine remained the same. Marv' never brought Gunz with him when he went to conduct business with Biggs because Gunz's reputation was well-known around the hood. His presence would put everyone on guard. On one particular day, however, Marv' allowed Gunz to accompany him.

Marv' went to meet up with Biggs and Trigg at 9:00pm. As usual, he was on time. Biggs and Trigg were already there waiting for him. Trigg always liked to show up early. He was distrusting of everyone and Marv' was no exception. He could care less how much money he brought in. He still didn't trust him.

Everything seemed to be business as usual as Marv' got out of his car. He gave dap to both men and proceeded to make small talk. The entire time, Marv' was a nervous wreck . He *knew* Trigg was a dangerous man and he was about to make the biggest move of his life that night. He was adhering to the 48 Laws of Power. He was *"entering into action with boldness."* He felt a little at ease knowing that 2-Gunz was in the trunk with his pistol grip riot pump shotgun. As the men made their way to the back of the car, Marv' said, "Let's get this money, baby!" giving the verbal signal and simultaneously smacked his hand down on the trunk.

Marv' inserted the key, lifted the trunk and stepped to the side. 2-Gunz sprang into action and blasted Trigger at point blank range in the face. The force from the shotgun slug tore half of Trigger's head off, making him unrecognizable even to those who knew him best. Biggs was caught totally off guard. He was so shocked, it never registered in his mind to try to escape or to even draw his gun. Gunz cocked the shotgun and shot Biggs in the chest.

He then climbed out of the trunk, chambered another round and shot Biggs in the head. Marv' retrieved the bag containing the kilo of dope, as well as the $60,000 he owed for the consignment of his last package. Overall, it was a nice score for him. The most important factor of the night, however, was the fact that Centre Ave would belong solely to him. From that day forth, Marv' would lay down the law of the land for Centre Ave. Anyone he felt may pose a problem to his rise, he would have Gunz kill them without warning.

***

Body and Psych were aware of Marv's history and the reputation of 2-Gunz. They had heard stories about him since they were kids. They knew it may be a problem moving in on Centre. Body voiced his concerns with the idea.

"I don't know if it's even worth it, Psych. Truthfully, I mean we got a good thing going, elsewhere. We got this wholesale game. We got these fire breezos flying out the door. Doesn't make any sense going after something that's uncertain. We can open the market somewhere else, where niggas are basically begging us to set up shop." said Body.

"Yeah, I feel you, but I want Centre. Fuck Marv! Fuck 2-Gunz and whoever else. Them niggas old and washed up. Their reign is over. Them niggas are soft. I'm telling you. Gunz is living off his reputation from back in the day. Don't nobody give a fuck about what you *used* to do nigga. That shit don't hold no weight. Gunz ain't bust his gun in over 10 years, probably. I'm what that nigga *used* to be and more. Fuck them niggas, Bro!" Psycho was fired up.

"Fuck it. This is what I propose. I say we offer to supply them niggas with birds at a reasonable number. If they decline, we put all the workers we can muster on the ave with dope *way* better than the shit they're slinging. Fuck it. It will be a get down or lay down thing, minus the muscle. If them niggas act stupid, then we flex. Either way, it's whatever!" said Body.

He wanted to avoid going to war, if possible. He knew a war would put a damper on the cashflow. He, also, knew that those things were sometimes necessary.

"Yeah, I like the sound of that. However, you wanna do it, my nigga. You already know how I'm coming. Let's see if they wanna do business, first. Then, we'll take it from there." responded Psych.

Chapter 10

Body was in a silver 2004 Dodge Intrepid. The game had been good to him since Mila plugged him in with Carlito. That was about 7 months ago. Since then, Body was able to stack a significant amount of money. Just a few months shy of his 18th birthday, he was almost a millionaire. He was now the proud owner of a pearl white Range Rover Supercharged, after trading in his Navigator. He, also, owned six other vehicles that he used for business purposes, including the Dodge Intrepid he was riding in. In addition, he had a red 2006 Ford Taurus, a white 2005 Nissan Altima, a black 2006 Nissan Maxima, a navy blue 2005 Dodge Minivan, and a tan 2006 Chrysler Sebring. All of his vehicles were equipped with tinted windows and stash boxes.

The most important thing Body was able to accomplish was buying a house in Squirrel Hill. This allowed him to move Jasmine and Robin out of the Section 8 townhouse in Oak Hill. He had always dreamt of being able to move his family. He was never a big fan of remaining on subsidized housing. His next plan of action was to move Mama Jones. She lived in a Section 8 townhouse on the Northside. She used to live on Burrows Street some years back before all of the reconstruction. Once the gentrification began, Mama Jones opted to move instead of waiting for the townhomes to be constructed and be forced out eventually. As soon as the money began pouring in for Body, he tried to convince Mama Jones to move, but she would hear nothing of it. She said that she was fine where she was and there were much more important things for Body to do with his money. She suggested that he should figure those things out. Those were the things on Body's mind as he navigated the Intrepid down Perrysville Ave on his way to visit Mama Jones.

He hadn't seen her in quite a while, over two months to be exact. He had been avoiding her. She had a way of making him feel guilty. Usually, he would never go so long without seeing her or communicating with her. He used to call her on a daily basis just to check on her. But, it had been far too long, so he decided to finally face her.

Body pulled over in front of Mama Jones house. He killed the engine and exited the car. Body made his way up the flight of cement stairs to his grandraise's house. She didn't have a garage. A lot of the homes on the Northside were built that way. There was a porch with a divider to separate it from the neighbor's house. He rang the doorbell.

Moments later, Mama Jones opened the door. Recognizing her grandbaby, she unlocked the screen door.

"Get in here, boy! Where you been?" Mama Jones asked.

Body entered the house and embraced his grandraise with a big hug. It was good to see her.

"You hungry, Baby? I got some black-eyed peas and cornbread in there and some grape koolaid. You still like grape Kool-Aid don't you, Baby?" asked Mama Jones.

Her anger with her grandson had subsided, instantaneously, when she saw him. She went straight into nurturing mode.

"Yes, Ma'am." said Body.

"Alright, hold on a second." said Mama Jones.

Mama Jones went into the kitchen and returned five minutes later carrying a tray containing a glass bowl of black-eyed peas with hammocks, a large piece of apple cinnamon cornbread and a glass of grape Kool-Aid.

"Here you go, Baby."

She passed the tray to Body. He began to dig into the food avoiding eye contact with Mama Jones.

"So, where you been, boy? You don't love ya grandmama, no mo'?" asked Mama Jones.

"Of course, I love you, grandma."

"Well, why haven't you been answering my calls?"

Still avoiding eye contact while he ate, Body lied, "I didn't get ya call."

"Now you need to stop fixing ya face to tell such lies, boy! I may be old, but I'm no damn fool!"

Mama Jones was always a straight shooter. She had never bitten her tongue for anyone and she wasn't about to start now.

"I know why you haven't been around here and I want to tell you, I don't like it! I don't like it one bit! I've raised you better than that! You should be ashamed of yourself, Jabar! I love you to death, but for the first time in my life, I can say that I'm ashamed of you."

This direct line of chastening from Mama Jones was killing Body. He was aware of how she felt about drugs and those who dealt them. They have had conversations about it before. But never has it been so intense. Never has she been ashamed of him. As he sat there and took the ear beating his grandraise was dishing out, it all became clear why Mama Jones was so infuriated.

"How the hell you gonna give drugs to ya own mama, Jabar?"

Body raised his head for the first time, since he came in the house and shockingly looked Mama Jones in her teary eyes.

"How could you?" asked Mama Jones

"I...I...I," Body began to stammer trying to figure out what to say.

"I, I, I, my ass! Don't say shit. Don't fix ya face to make up some bullshit excuse or tell another lie in this house! I want you to get out of this house. Get out and don't you show up on this doorstep, again. Until you get your shit together and start acting like the man I raised you to be!"

She was infuriated all over, again. As happy as she was to see him after his hiatus, she couldn't bear the sight of him at the moment.

Feeling crushed, Body rose from the couch with a look of defeat. Every time he visited his grandraise, he left cash for her to take care of all her necessities, plus extra money for whatever she wanted to use it for. This time would be no different, or so he thought. As Body stood to leave, he reached into his pocket and pulled out a wad of cash. He peeled off $1,000 in all one hundred dollar bills and extended his hand, attempting to give the money to Mama Jones. Much to his dismay, she declined his generosity.

"If that's the demon that looms over our family and is responsible for our separation, I don't want any part of it."

Body left Mama Jones house feeling down, but also confused about how she knew what he had been doing. He reached in the arm rest compartment and pulled out a half-smoked blunt. He inhaled the weed and held it as long as he could before releasing a thick cloud of smoke and pungent odor into the car's interior. He pulled away from the curb with his head in a fog.

Chapter 11

P sycho was cruising down Fifth Avenue in a black SRT8 Cherokee. He was in search of one of his workers. Fifth Avenue was a long strip. It stretched out a few miles. It ran from Oakland through the Hill District and into downtown. However, all of the hoeing and drug dealing were confined to a few blocks radius. It was a one way street that consisted of three lanes, one of which was entirely devoted as a bus lane going in the opposite direction. Fifth Ave received a lot of foot traffic, due to the plethora of businesses. The strip was ripe for prostitutes from all over the city to work. Naturally, it was a good place to set up a drug organization and Psycho decided to set up shop.

Fifth Avenue ran parallel to Forbes Avenue. There was an alley that separated the two avenues through the entire stretch on the Hill District. This was perfect for Psycho. He got a place on Forbes Avenue that would be used for packaging and storing the product. His workers wouldn't have to travel on the main street to get up and down the avenue. They would use the alley, instead.

Not seeing the guy he was looking for, Psycho made a left turn then another left onto the alley between Fifth and Forbes. He pulled over in front of the trap house and entered through the back door. When he entered the house, he noticed that four of his workers were there. All of which were his or Body's cousins.

"Why ain't nobody outside?" asked Psych.

"We had to put some more shit together. All that other shit we had is finished." said Moose.

"Ya'll sold the 300 breezos, I left here last night?" asked a surprised Psycho.

"Yeah, that shit is gone." responded Moose.

"It's biting out there, Psych." said Menace.

Menace was the youngest out of the group at 15 years old. He was Body's first cousin. They usually left Menace in the house on table duty because he was so young. Body and Psycho wanted to give Menace a chance to earn some money, so he could buy himself some clothes and sneaks. Also, in the house were Pitbull and Man Man. Man Man was the eldest of the crew at 22 years old. He was in charge of the operation whenever Psych or Body weren't around. He managed the workers and stash houses. Man Man was the first cousin of Psycho, but he had a closer relationship with Body.

"I called Body last night when we started running low on work. He came through with 500 grams that were already cut. So, we just had to bag it. We got about 300 finished, right now." said Man Man.

"Cool. Menace, I want you and Man Man to stay here and finish putting the rest of that work together. Moose and Pitbull... I want ya'll to get started with that 300. I need *Obsession* to ring bells all over the city. When ya'll done, we going to *The Laga* tonight. Shit is picking up and we need to do a little celebrating. Be ready around 11:00." said Psych.

Everyone was excited about going out. They all had pockets full of money and they were sure there would be plenty of women to choose from. *The Laga* was a nightclub located in the Oakland area of

Pittsburgh. This particular area was a business district. It maintained a heavy flow of traffic throughout the day and into the wee hours of the morning. *The Laga* required all males to be 21 or older for entry, but the females could get in at 18. The bar area was sectioned off to prevent underage drinking. It was a futile tactic because the girls who wanted admittance to the bar would just mark the back of their own hands to pass the fluorescent light test. So essentially, you had a club full of tipsy young girls, who were ripe for the picking.

Everything went well on the block. By the time 11:00 pm had rolled around, Man Man had facilitated the movement of more than 400 breezos. Body and Psycho rode back-to-back in their Range Rovers as they picked up the crew. Body's Range was pearl white and Psycho's was black. They drove through the back alleys until they reached the spot and picked up everyone, except Menace. Menace didn't have any ID and looked too young to get in, so he stayed in the crib and played Xbox.

When they arrived at the club, they had to park in the parking garage around the corner. There weren't any parking spaces for as far as the eye could see. Once they made it to the front door of the club, they greased the palms of the bouncers to bypass the long line stretching down the block. As usual, the club was packed. The crew made their way to the caged in bar area to have a few drinks and watch the thick girls dance provocatively on stage. Body pulled Psycho to the side out of earshot of the rest of the crew, so they could talk.

"What's good?" asked Psych.

"Yo, I like how shit is picking up on the ave, Ike. But, I think we should reorganize it a lil' bit. I was thinking about getting another spot on Forbes, a couple blocks down from where we are. It's safer and keeps niggas off the streets." said Body.

"We can try it and see how it works." said Psycho.

As the men concluded their conversation, they heard the DJ announce the last call for alcohol. They enjoyed a few more drinks, talked to a few more ladies, then departed the club. It was nearly 3:00 am, but *The Laga* didn't officially close until 3:30 am. Their reason for leaving early was to get something to eat.

"I need something on my stomach to support this alcohol." said Moose.

"Let's go to Dirty O's." said Man Man.

Everybody agreed and they all began walking to *Originals Diner*. *Originals*, better known as "Dirty O's", was a few blocks away from *The Laga*. With nowhere to park due to the open bars and University of Pittsburgh's fraternity and sorority parties, the men had to leave their vehicles in the parking garage.

Originals was a two-story diner with a bar on the second floor. The first floor had a wrap around counter extending from one side of the establishment to the other. They served everything from pizza, chicken platters, battered shrimp, hot dogs and an assortment of other food and beverages. *Originals* earned the nickname "Dirty O's" because of its dingy interior and filthy bathrooms. It was, also, rumored that they didn't change the grease they used to cook the food. Nevertheless, "Dirty O's" was a goldmine! It was packed beyond capacity every weekend and maintained a healthy flow of traffic during the week, as well. "Dirty O's" stayed open until 6:00 am and reopened around 8:30 am. On the weekends, it would get so crowded, the police would lock the doors, so no one else could enter. They would walk up and down the street with their K-9's making people leave the area. This was another reason the crew left early. They had to get to the "O" before it got too packed.

As they stepped outside the club, they noticed the police barricading points of entry and directing traffic out of Oakland.

"Damn. Every time Black people get together they treat us like criminals and animals. Look at this shit! This is some bullshit! You got the White boys right around the corner from here smashing bottles and wilding in the street. *Nobody ever fucks with them.* If too many Blacks get together, it's a red flag and a reason to put the riot gear on." said Body.

He was referring to the police cruiser sitting in the intersection with its lights flashing. Body was disgusted at this point.

"Let's hurry up, before these pigs try locking the doors at the O." said Psycho.

When they arrived at *Originals*, it was crowded, but they were able to find a table. Within twenty minutes of their arrival, the spot was so packed that it was difficult to move. There were crowds of people standing shoulder to shoulder. The police locked the doors to prevent more people from entering.

"Aint that shit a fire hazard? How the fuck we supposed to get out of this bitch, if a fire breaks out? This shit is crazy." said Body.

The men's orders of chicken platters and x-large tub of fries had arrived. One x-large tub of fries at *Originals* was enough to feed all six men.

"Man, it's crowded as hell in here. Let's go upstairs." said Moose.

"Hell yeah." replied Pitbull.

The crew grabbed up their food and slowly made their way to the stairs, scooting between the throng of patrons. It was a lot less crowded upstairs. They took seats near the window to see the streets out front. As they laughed, joked, ate, and discussed business, something from the corner of Psycho's eye caught his attention.

"Yo, Body! Ain't that the nigga, 2-Gunz, right there?"

Body turned to his left and looked across the bar. Sure enough, there was not only 2-Gunz, but Marv' as well. They were also accompanied by two other guys.

"Yeah, that's him. And that's Marv' with the tan bucket hat on."

"Let's go holla at them niggas, now and see what's up."

"Aight, bet." responded Body.

Body and Psych rose from the table and made their way over to the group of men.

"Heads up. Who are these niggas heading this way?" 2-Gunz asked his crew.

Everyone turned and looked in the direction of Body and Psycho as they approached. The two unidentified men slid their hands in their waistband to clutch the butt of their automatic weapons. They were prepared for a confrontation, should one ensue.

"What's good?" said Body, addressing Marv' and extending his hand as a pleasantry. "I'm Body and this is my man, Psycho." said Body.

Marv' nodded his head and accepted the handshake from Body, while wondering who he was and what he wanted.

"We're from the Hill, Burrows street. I have some business that I'd like to discuss with you. It's sure to be lucrative for both of us." said Body.

"What kind of business you talking about, young blood?" asked 2-Gunz.

"Ain't nobody talking to you." said Psycho, rudely.

He didn't like 2-Gunz and wasn't trying to hide it. Psycho felt like 2-Gunz was a washed up old-head. He was hoping these niggas didn't see shit Body's way, so he could apply pressure. 2-Gunz picked up on Psycho's energy and the two locked eyes.

"Nigga, if you got something to discuss, it goes through me. Otherwise, it don't go through." said 2-Gunz.

His voice boomed and his agitation showed. This put a smile on Psycho's face.

"Look, let's just calm down. We ain't come here for that." said Body.

"Well, what you come here for?" asked 2-Gunz, addressing Body, but still locking eyes with a smirking Psycho.

"We came here to do business. We got birds of raw heroin that are more potent than anything the city has ever seen. Right now, we have bricks out there called *Obsession*, that's ringing bells. It's the best in the city. I figured we should do business together and lock everything down. This is the kind of dope that can bring Centre Ave back to its heyday." said Body.

"Man, you lil niggas got some nerve." started 2-Gunz, before he was cut off by Marv'.

"We appreciate the offer, but we'll pass. See you guys later."
said Marv'.

And just like that, Body was shut down with a dismissive wave.
With that, Body and Psycho turned to leave, but not before Psycho
could throw some fuel in the fire. He looked 2-Gunz in the eyes and
said, "You should try to stay calm, so you don't catch a heart attack or
stroke or some shit old head!"

Psycho walked away laughing, already devising a scheme in his
mind. He rounded up his crew and departed *Originals*. Once they were
outside Psycho laid out his plans.

"Pitbull and Moose, I want ya'll to get a couple niggas and hit
Centre Ave this morning. By 6:00 a.m., I want yall handing out samples
of *Obsession*. Don't sell that shit! Not a single bag. I'm gonna give ya'll
fifty breezos to pass out. Every single bag is *free*. We shutting that shit
down ASAP. Fuck them old niggas!" Psycho looked at his watch. It
read 4:30 a.m.

As the crew was leaving *Originals*, 2-Gunz walked over to the
window and looked out onto the street. He watched the crew until they
disappeared around the corner. Then, he walked back over to his own
crew at the bar.

"I got a bad feeling about that lil' nigga. I might have to
chastise his lil' ass." he said.

"Excuse that shit. Them lil' niggas ain't no threat. They're
starting to make a couple dollars and they're smelling their own ass
now. They ain't no threat! Drink up nigga. Fuck that." said Marv'.

Chapter 12

At six o'clock sharp, Moose, Pitbull, and two of their homeboys had set up shop on Centre Avenue in front of *Wongs*. It was a small, hole in the wall, convenience store owned by some Koreans. Moose decided to enlist the help of Stickman and Taliban.

Stickman was possibly the best driver on the east coast. Let him tell it, he was the best in the world. His driving record had been impeccable since he was 11 years old. Once he was behind the wheel of a car, forget about it. There was no catching him. Plus, they didn't make many cars that he couldn't steal. His favorite being Cherokees and Audis. Moose felt it would be good to bring him along, in case he got in a jam. Stickman was parked across the street in the driver's seat of Psycho's black Cherokee SRT8, watching the scene. Taliban was, also, a good driver. Although, he had nothing on Stickman. However, Taliban was a shooter. At 17 years old, he was a certified head buster. If he had a problem with a guy, he would shoot instead of fight. He got a rush every time he had a gun in his hand. When he arrived on Centre, he was equipped with a Glock .357 with an extended clip that Psycho had given him. Taliban was hoping someone would give him a reason to use it. He stood a few paces from Moose and Pitbull as they gave out free bags of *Obsession*. Crowds of addicts were lining up to get their free hit. A lot of fiends tried to get in line more than once, but were abruptly turned away.

Because of the large turnout, some of the fiends were able to make it through the line multiple times unnoticed. Many people came back to buy *Obsession,* but were told it wouldn't be available for purchase until later. They were redirected to go to Fifth ave to get it. A little after 8 o'clock, the fifty bricks had been passed out. With no other reason to stick around, Moose, Pitbull, and Taliban got in the jeep with Stickman and pulled off.

Moose called Psycho to keep him abreast on the situation. He wanted to inform him that the plan had been completed without a hitch.

"Yo," answered Psycho on the third ring.

"What's poppin', Ike? We finished that." said Moose.

"How did it go?" asked Psycho.

"Smooth. I'll tell you more when I see you."

"Aight, meet me in Oakland in the CVS parking lot." said Psycho.

"Bet," said Moose and he disconnected the call.

Eight minutes later, they arrived at the scheduled destination. They waited twenty more minutes before Psycho finally arrived driving his black Dodge Durango. All four youth jumped out of the jeep to greet Psycho and show their respect.

"Yo, that shit got a Hemi in it?" asked Stickman. He was referring to the Durango that Psycho was driving. Psycho looked back at the truck then back at Stickman.

"Yeah, that shit got a Hemi. But on another note, what's good with that business?" asked Psycho.

"Man, they loved that shit! We need to get something popping ASAP." said Pitbull.

"Aight, let's make it happen. I was at the spot when ya'll called. There's 500 breezos waiting for ya'll, right now. So, go get what ya'll need and make it slap." Psycho said.

"Bet." Moose replied.

Everybody gave Psycho dap before piling back into the Cherokee. They headed to the spot and picked up 200 of the 500 bricks. Body was there, when they arrived.

"What's good?" Body greeted everyone.

"What's up?" They responded in unison.

"We came to get some work. We bout to make shit slap on Centre." Moose said.

"Aight, but if ya'll going up there, I wanna make sure ya'll aight. Ya'll can't just be standing around with all that work. I'll go with ya'll." said Body.

The men left the trap house and headed towards Centre. Moose and the rest of the men got into the Cherokee and Body got into his black Maxima.

Arriving on Centre Ave, Body pulled over in front of Doc's corner store. Doc was an old-head around 75 years old. He owned his store since some time in the 1970's, when Centre Ave *was* Centre Ave. That was before the riots. It was a hole-in-the-wall joint, but it was Mr. Doc's pride and joy. Doc was a business owner at a time when not many Black people owned anything besides the clothes on their backs.

Doc knew Body since he was a baby coming into the store with Mama Jones. When he was younger, Body used to think Doc was weird because he would tell everybody that he loved them. Anytime someone made a purchase, he would say, "Thank you, young man. Come again, young man. I love you, young man."

Over the years, Body became accustomed to it. When he walked into the store, Doc was sitting on a crate behind the dusty glass counter reading a copy of the *Pittsburgh Courier*. It was Pittsburgh's only black newspaper. Body hadn't been in Doc's store in quite some time, but things hadn't changed since the last time he was there. The interior of the store was still drab and had very limited supplies.

Body walked over to the counter, "What's up, old timer?"

Doc looked up at Body through squinted eyes, "Jabar?"

"Yeah, it's me."

"Boy, I ain't seen you since you was yay high." said Doc holding his hand at waist level for emphasis.

"How you been, son?" asked Doc.

"I've been good."

"How's that grandmother of yours?"

"She's doing good, too."

"You tell her I said hi. Ya hear?"

"Aight, Doc. I'll tell her."

Still feeling guilty about the last conversation he had with his grandraise, Body changed the subject. "How's business going, Doc?"

"Well, it's slow as usual, but it's still *mine.*"

"Well, that's what I came to talk to you about today. Business. I have a lil' something set up here on Centre and I need ya help. Before I get into details, I want you to know that I'll make it worth your while."

"What do you need me to do?" asked Doc.

"I need you to hold onto something for me until my people come to get it. And I need you to put a safe behind the counter."

"Alright, youngster. Don't sound too difficult."

"Good." Body said as he dug into his pocket and retrieved a wad of bills. He peeled off $2,000 and handed it to Doc, who accepted the cash with lust-filled bulging eyes. Body then grabbed a pencil and piece of paper to write down his contact info.

"Any questions or problems, call me." Body said as he handed the piece of paper to Doc.

"Will do." said a happy Doc.

Body stepped into the entrance of the door and waved Moose over to the store. Moose emerged from the jeep carrying a footlocker bag. Body made the introduction between the two. Then, he passed Doc the footlocker bag containing 190 bricks. The other 10 bricks would be distributed across the street. Body wanted to minimize his risk, so he didn't want the crew to have too much product on them at any given time. He assured Mr. Doc that a safe would be arriving the next day.

Once everything was established, Body said his goodbyes and departed the store.

***

2-Gunz was sitting at a traffic light on Centre, next to the public library. He was driving a black Cadillac Escalade adorned with 24" rims. The light turned green and he drove straight ahead past the Zone

2 Police Station. He made a right turn, and then a quick left into the alley running parallel behind Centre Ave. He came to a halt at a small almost dilapidated looking house. This house was the basis of his Centre Avenue operation. He climbed out of the truck and was greeted by Junior. Junior was one of 2-Gunz workers. He had known Junior ever since he was a baby and considered him family. That was the primary reason for Gunz putting Junior in charge of Centre's daily operations.

"What's up, June?"

"Ain't shit. Just chilling. Trying to get this paper right. Shit kinda slow out here."

"Well, it'll pick up. You know how it is sometimes. Just give me what you got." said Gunz.

Junior reached into his pocket and gave Gunz the few thousand dollars he managed to accumulate. Usually, these pickups would net more money and required a bag. Today, it was all in one pocket.

"I guess it's *real* slow." Gunz commented, as he looked at the bills Junior passed him.

"Next time you come through, shit should be straight."

"Aight, bet." Gunz replied.

With that, he climbed back into his Escalade and pulled away from the curb. At the first intersection, he made a left turn going down hill and rested at a stop sign. Signaling right onto Centre Ave, something across the street caught Gunz's attention. Body was getting into a black Maxima. Gunz recognized him as the youngster from *Originals*. He took his presence as a coincidence. He had never noticed him before. But he knew once there was a confrontation, however slight, you would never forget the other person's face, again. If he continued to see him, he would deal with it then. *That was the difference between him and Psycho.* Psycho would have shot him and lived with the consequences. He was under the belief *"it's better to be alive and wrong, than dead and right"*. He didn't want to find himself in a situation, where he was on the ground bleeding out because he didn't follow his instincts about a nigga.

***

Back at the trap house, Psycho was playing NBA Live on the Playstation 3 when Body came through the door.

"What's popping?"

"What's good?" responded Psycho.

Menace was at the table bagging up dope with four females who were recently employed.

"Just coming through to check up on shit. It's slapping on Centre. I got some plans that should help reign in control."

"What you got in mind?" asked Psycho.

"Well, you know how you like to say we need eyes and ears?" Body said.

"Yeah." responded Psych, all while never taking his eyes from the game that he was engaged in.

"Well, I got shit set up, so that old man Doc is gonna hold the work for us and put a safe behind the counter. I was thinking, we should invest in his store. Fix that shit up. Put cameras in the store, even outside the store. Imagine the ability to watch everything happening on the ave. Shit, if it works the way I imagine, we'll duplicate it everywhere. We can access the cameras from the computer."

"Damn nigga, you a genius!" exclaimed Psycho.

"We can watch everything from right here! As long as we're on the same page about that, we might as well put up cameras around the trap house, so we can watch the alley, too." said Body.

"Hell yeah. I'm with that."

"Plus, we can move this set up in the basement and put cameras down there, too." Body said referring to the system they had for bagging up dope.

"I'll get on top of all that shit today, so we can have it installed by tomorrow." said Body.

With that, he was on his way out the door.

***

The next day, Mila was up bright and early. Body had given her the task of seeing things through with the cameras at Doc's, as well as the cameras around the trap house overlooking the alley.

Mila arranged for the contractors to begin work on Doc's store that morning. She would have everything remodeled, floors, walls, ceilings and doors. No stone would be left unturned. There would be new shelves installed. A new countertop, surrounded by bulletproof glass. The whole project would be complete in 33 days. It was a complete renovation, afterall. Mila was in the trap house watching the computer guy as he set everything up for internet access on the new *MacBook* she had bought that morning. It was only to be used for illicit purposes, never for personal things, like banking or *social media.*

By noon, all the cameras were set up and able to be viewed via the computer. She directed the workers to Centre Avenue and had the same system installed outside of Doc's store. She couldn't have the system installed on the inside until the renovations were complete. The installation company chose strategic places for the cameras based on the client's needs. When they were finished, Body would be able to watch a large section of the avenue. When Mila brought it home for his final consent, he was pleased with her work. This put a big smile on her face. She was a pleaser. *If she satisfied her man, she received satisfaction in knowing it.*

"That's why I love you girl."

"¡Te amo también, Papi!"[18] was her response as she leaned over and kissed him.

They had been together for the better part of a year and everything seemed perfect. They bought a house together in Penn Hills that had four bedrooms, two and half bathrooms, a pool and a Jacuzzi. Body was happy with his accomplishments, but he still saw a lot of room for improvement. He wanted it all... fast cars, diamonds, mansions, a boatload of money *and the boat to go with it.* He wouldn't rest until he had it.

"You like the house, Baby?" He asked her.

---

[18] I love you too, Papi!

"Of course, I love this house, Papi. Why you ask me that, you don't like it?"

"I mean, yeah, I like it. It's aight for now. Eventually, I'll want better. Plus, you might want one of them *lil' Mexican casitas*[19]."

He laughed as he teased her about Spanish style homes.

"Oh, you got jokes?" Mila said in her Jersey accent. She playfully mushed Body's head.

"Seriously though Papi, you gotta take ya time. You've accomplished a lot of things in a short amount of time. Things, some people will never accomplish. You gotta slow down. Bad things happen when people speed. It's gonna be okay, Papi. Just stay focused."

"Don't worry, Baby I'm focused. Focused on that fat ass you got!"

He playfully slapped her on the ass. She turned around to face him as he sat on the couch. She straddled his lap and kissed him passionately. He began to peel off her clothes.

---

[19] Little houses

Chapter 13

2-Gunz pulled over at his trap house to collect the daily take. The money had been short all week and it was beginning to annoy him. He jumped out of the Escalade as Junior was coming out of the house. He had the same dumb look on his face that he had been having lately. It was a look that told Gunz there still wasn't any good news.

"What's up, Gunz?" said Junior.

"You tell me, June."

"*Same shit.* Ain't no money coming through. I only made $600 since yesterday but…"

He was abruptly cut off by the boom of 2-Gunz's voice.

"Nigga! You tryna play me? You don't think I've been around long enough to know the game?" he said in an accusatory tone.

Junior was clearly hurt by his words. He had always been loyal to Gunz. He had never stolen a red cent or did any unauthorized business. So, he couldn't understand why he was being confronted like that by his mentor.

"Look Gunz, I don't know what you're trying to imply, but you know me better than that, my nigga. I would never be on no bullshit with you. If I would've had a chance, I was about to tell you that I know why shit been going so slow."

"*Well nigga*, don't keep me waiting in suspense! What's up?"

"Somebody put some different work on the strip. I knew something was going on when I walked to *Wong's* to buy some blunts and shit. There was a big ass crowd out that bitch looking like zombies. They were all in line to buy this." said June.

He dug into his pocket and retrieved a white glassine wax bag with a red stamp. Junior passed it to 2-Gunz. 2-Gunz took the bag and examined it. The name stamped across the bag was murmured in a whisper… *Obsession?* He looked at Junior with a puzzled look on his face, trying to recall where he had heard the name before.

"I know this name from somewhere."

"Yeah, me too." said Junior.

Gunz looked Junior in the eyes as he awaited an explanation.

"Remember, a couple weeks ago, the night we all went to *Originals?*"

"Yeah, what about it?"

"Well, 'member the niggas that approached us? Well not us, but they approached you and Marv' about some business. They said something about having shit on smash with *Obsession* and how we should get down." Junior reminded him.

It all started to become clear to Gunz. It made sense. The confrontation at *Originals*, the shortage of money *and* customers, all since running into Body and Psycho. They must've made their move around the time he saw Body leaving Doc's store. Gunz's face was etched with tension. He was kicking himself for not foreseeing the move and running down on Body the day he saw him on Centre. He was unaware that Body was trained to go. Plus, he had a truckful of hitters with him. He would've been aired out had he tried *anything.*

"Nah, fuck that! We shutting them niggas down ASAP. Take care of that shit, June!" said Gunz.

"You know them niggas ain't out there pumping that shit themselves." June said.

"I don't give a fuck *who's* out there! Make sure they're not out there no more!"

Junior made a call to his man, Livewire. They grew up together in G-Block. When it was time to put in work, Livewire was the one person June could trust other than Gunz. 2-Gunz had already given the order. June knew what had to be done. It wouldn't be the first time, he had put a nigga down.

June told Livewire to meet him at the trap house ASAP to discuss the business at hand. G-Block projects sat over Centre Ave, so it took Livewire less than five minutes to walk to the trap house. When he arrived, June explained the situation, with what he called "the new kids on the block", and how he planned to take care of it.

"Aight, when you wanna handle this shit?" asked Livewire.

"Tonight. But, I need you to get the ski masks and gear ready." said June.

"All I need is a black t-shirt. As soon as it gets dark outside, we'll move on them niggas."

"But, right now I want you to walk around the corner to *Wong's* and peep the set up. I want you to get a good look at them niggas. You can't miss 'em. They're pumping real hard. Just go around there and cop some blunts or something."

Livewire walked down the hill and made a right onto Centre. As he walked past the Jitney station, he noticed a large crowd. In the midst of junkies, he saw two young boys handling the crowd. One was collecting the money. The other was passing out the product. Livewire scanned the scene and noticed Stickman in the Cherokee parked across the street. He wouldn't have noticed him through the dark tint, except Stickman had the driver side window rolled down. He noticed that Stickman seemed to be scanning the area, too. Livewire figured he was either watching the young boys back or he was scheming.

He went inside the store and bought two vanilla dutches. Then, headed back to the spot. Upon arrival, he filled June in on everything he saw. From there, they devised a plan.

"If that car is still out there tonight, you take care of the driver as soon as I start hitting them other clowns. You just gotta find a way to get close enough, so the nigga can't jump out the car blazing or alert the other niggas, before I get in position." June said.

"I got this, my nigga."

***

"Damn, this shit is crazy. I ain't never seen this much gwap!" said Moose.

"Hell yeah," replied Pitbull.

Him, Moose and Stickman rotated two blunts around in a cipher. They were taking a smoke break since they had put in heavy hours on the block. It was the 15th of the month, *a day favored by all hustlers*. It was the day that checks were being cut all over the city. It was payday! It was sure to be a prosperous day for most.

Psycho had already come through and collected the money for the shift. It came out to be a little over $40,000. Centre Ave was beginning to surpass everyone's expectations in a short period of time.

"Man, I'm hungry as a mafucka!" said Pitbull.

"Hell yeah." agreed Moose.

"Let's go get something to eat." Stickman chimed in.

"Shit, you see all them fiends across the street nigga. We gotta finish getting this gwap." Moose retorted.

"Yeah, just grab us something and swing back through." said Pitbull.

"Aight. Imma go to *Wendy's* on the boulevard. What ya'll want?" Stickman asked.

"Let me get four bacon cheeseburgers, some biggie fries, and a biggie frostie." said Moose.

"Damn, you some greedy ass nigga." Stickman retorted.

"I want two of those chicken joints with bacon and french dressing on it, and two biggie fries, a frosty and a sprite." said Pitbull.

"You gonna remember all this shit?" asked Moose.

"Yeah, nigga. I'm high not stupid."

"Aight, bet." said Pitbull.

He and Moose departed the Jeep.

"A yo, Stick! Don't forget to get ketchup and no onions on my shit!" yelled Moose.

"Aight." Stick said as he pulled away from the curb in route of Baum Blvd.

Pitbull and Moose headed back across the street to take care of their awaiting clientele. The duo was high out of their minds from the two blunts of sour diesel they just smoked. Besides the task at hand of serving the fiends, they were totally oblivious to everything else going on around them, including the two men peeking from around the corner of the Jitney station.

June and Livewire stood at the corner surveying the strip. They were looking for police presence and the Jeep Livewire spotted earlier.

"I don't see no Jeep."

"I don't see it either. Maybe the nigga bounced." said Livewire.

"Aight, fuck it." June said as he checked the chamber of the Glock .40 to make sure there was a round in the head.

He pulled his ski mask down over his face and began to creep towards the young boys and crowd of fiends. Livewire followed close behind. When they were close enough, they pushed their way through the crowd and were face to face with the young boys.

Pitbull looked up at the confusion going on in the crowd, expecting to see some antsy customer. But instead, he was looking down the barrel of June's Glock. His wide eyes registered the shock he felt before the barrel of the gun exploded in his face sending a sharp pain to the right side of his head. The other five shots came in rapid succession, but Pitbull only felt the first, which killed him instantly.

Moose made an attempt to pull his gun and assist his cousin, but never had a chance. His futile attempt was met by an excruciating pain to his chest from the .44 Magnum that Livewire hit him with. The sound of the cannon booming was deafening to everyone in close proximity. As Moose fell to his knees, Livewire shot him three more times. Once in the hand as Moose reached for the gun in self defense and twice more in the chest. The powerful kick of the .44 caused

Livewire's arm to jerk violently upwards with each shot fired. The crowd of fiends had dispersed after the first shot was fired. Some of them taking cover behind parked cars.

June and Livewire took off running, on their way to G-block. They didn't want to risk anyone seeing them running to the trap house. Instead, they went to the projects to lay low for the rest of the night. As soon as they took flight, the fiends swarmed the dead bodies, like vultures on carnage. They searched their corpses for money and, most importantly, bags of *Obsession*. After stripping the two dead bodies of all their valuables, the fiends disappeared into thin air before the cops could arrive.

Zone 2 Police Station was located only blocks away from the scene. Yet, it took approximately fifteen minutes before the first responding officer arrived. That's just how it was in the hood. Police were slow to respond to any disturbance that wasn't a bank robbery or another crime disturbing the city's *White peace*.

***

When police finally arrived on the scene, the uniformed officers began their work of keeping the crowd back. They did this in an effort to prevent the crime scene from becoming contaminated. Next, to arrive on the scene were EMT workers. They scurried over to the victims and made their pronouncement D.O.A., dead on arrival. The officers reported the declaration of the victim's status and requested the coroner as the Homicide Unit arrived on the scene.

The lead detective was an older black man by the name of Richard Collins. He was of average height, standing at 5' 9". He had a pot-belly, and his hairline was receding dramatically, but he insisted on holding onto it. The first thing Collins did was question the first responding officer to the scene to find out how much intel had been discovered. Next, he began re-questioning some onlookers standing around. He ordered the officers to canvas the scene for clues, particularly shell casings that may supply fingerprints. Collins' interrogation of the witnesses proved to be frivolous. Everyone claimed not to have seen or heard a thing.

"Excuse me, detective! We've got something over here." said a uniformed officer.

Collins excused himself from the woman he was questioning. He figured it must be something good, if the young officer pulled him away from a potential witness.

"What is it?"

"There it is." the officer said while pointing at the three shell casings discovered.

Collins pulled an ink pen from his inside jacket pocket. He used the tip of the pen to insert into the opening of the shell case to inspect it without contamination.

"This is a .40 caliber shell." said Collins.

"We've got a couple more a few feet away." said the officer.

Collins inspected the shell casings and guessed they would have all been discharged from the same firearm or at least the same caliber of firearm. He had the shells properly bagged and processed to be sent to the lab for further examination. Detective Collins then began to examine the bodies themselves. He noticed that one of the victims had a bullet hole just below the right eye. *His head had swelled.* He pulled out his small pocket notebook and began jotting feverishly as his partner, Detective John Novak, approached looking inquisitively over his shoulder.

Novak was a middle aged chain-smoker, who had been on the force nearly 25 years. He was a three time divorcee with a 27 year-old daughter from his second marriage *to Theresa. He hated Theresa.* He stood 5'11" with a head full of silver hair, a potbelly and a nasty spray tan that gave him an orange hue. His voice was raspy from years of Pall Malls.

"What you got there, partner?" he asked Collins.

"Well, we got two stiffs, D.O.A. GSW to the head on this one here."

He used a laser point pen to show his partner the gunshot wound underneath Pitbull's right eye.

"A .40 caliber… I'm thinking Glock. There's no IDs, so we have to fingerprint them at the morgue. Two black males, mid through late teens. No money, no jewelry, missing sneakers, ripped pockets… looks like a robbery." said Collins as he scribbled on his notepad.

"Look at that," said Novak.

He squatted down next to one of the bodies and used his pen to indicate the left earlobe of one John Doe. He pulled out a small pen flashlight to get a better look.

"Hmmm, looks like some sort of small laceration." said Novak.

"No! This kid had an earring and somebody snatched it out." said Collins.

As he was finishing his sentence, the cadavers were being loaded into black body bags and placed in the coroner's van.

***

Stickman stood amongst the crowd of onlookers at a scene that brought tears to his eyes. He made it there just in time to identify the bodies that were being zipped up in the body bags. On the way back from his *Wendy's* trip, Stick was driving down Centre Ave and he noticed a heavy police presence in the vicinity where he left Moose and Pitbull.

The police had the street blocked off. Their flashing lights could be seen bouncing off buildings for blocks. Stickman pulled over and walked toward the area where he left his homies. He was hoping they hadn't been arrested. But once he got to the scene, he wasn't prepared for what he was about to see. Sorrow filled Stickman's heart as he pulled out his cell phone and made a dreaded call.

"Hello, Psych? I got bad news, Bro."

***

The next morning 2 -Gunz was ecstatic to receive the news about *not one,* but two niggas getting *spanked* last night. *Spanked,* was the terminology associated with murder in Pittsburgh. It took over for *murked, bodied* and *slumped.* Either way, once 2 -Gunz discovered the death of the two youth, he felt a surge of excitement and decided to make a phone call, right away. A quarter after six in the morning, he was at home on the couch, wearing a tank top and navy blue boxers. He was tuned into *Fox 53* news. The broadcast made him stall his call. On the screen, he saw *exactly what* he was looking for. The news reporter began reporting on the story of the day:

> *"Good morning. I'm here in the 2200 block of Centre Avenue where approximately 7 hours ago, around 11pm last night, two teenage boys were slain in horrific fashion. Police are not releasing all the details. But from what we were able to gather, it appeared to be a robbery. Police aren't releasing the identity of the victims and have no suspects at this time. Police are asking, if **anyone** has information about this homicide, please call the number on your screen. This is Pam Costello reporting live from Fox 53 news. Back to you Pat."*

2-Gunz wasn't interested in hearing anything further. He was already on the phone calling June.

"Hello? What's good? Everything aight?" asked 2-Gunz, sounding like the nervous one.

"Yup, everything straight. I'm in the hood right now. I was gonna call you, but I didn't wanna wake you up." said June.

"Shit, with news like this, I don't mind. I been up for a few anyway. What time you getting up?" asked 2-Gunz.

"Shit, a better question is what time am I going to bed? I ain't sleep a wink last night." said June.

"Well, ain't no time for sleeping now. We got shit to discuss. Meet me at the spot at 10 and bring Livewire."

Chapter 14

Body and Psycho assembled the gang at Body's Penn Hills home. Stickman, Taliban, Man Man, and Menace were all in attendance. They sat around the computer in the dining room and watched as Mila navigated through the software. She was uploading the footage captured by the camera's placed outside of Doc's store. Everyone waited, with grave anticipation, as images of Centre Avenue popped onto the screen. Mila fast-forwarded the footage until she found what she was looking for.

The system recorded time and date, which was displayed on the bottom right corner of the screen. She played the footage, starting at 10:45 pm. They watched as Moose and Pitbull exited the Cherokee and Stickman pulled off. At 10:50 pm, they watched as two men crept toward Centre Avenue from the alley. Both were wearing ski masks. The masks were rolled up on their heads to resemble skully hats. It was the simplest way to protect their identity. When it was time for action, they would simply roll down the mask. However, they were unaware of the presence of cameras. The hightech resolution of the cameras would reveal *the whole truth and nothing, but the truth. Their secret couldn't remain hidden.*

"Rewind it and zoom in on their faces." Body commanded.

Mila zoomed in on the shooters making their identities clear. Psycho's voice cuts through the silence.

"I *fucking* knew it! I knew it! Those are the same niggas from the O who were with Marv' and that bitch ass nigga Gunz! I swear to God on my raise, I'm spanking them niggas!" Psycho yelled.

He was infuriated. Everyone was.

Three days after the murders, June was back in the trap house and had the strip popping, once again. He was able to fulfill the void created in the disappearance of Moose and Pitbull. The plan was for Man Man and Taliban to switch shifts with Moose and Pitbull, but in the wake of the deaths everyone was at a standstill.

Meanwhile, June was pumping hard. He was happy to have his cash flow back. He stood amongst a crowd of fiends who could rival any zombie from the walking dead. June was consumed by the bulging of his pockets. The large assortment of small bills made him feel richer than he actually was. He paid little attention to the two shabby, dreadlock wearing fiends on either side of him. His only concern was trying to count the fistful of fives he had been given. But had he been alert, he may have recognized the look of death in their eyes. After a brief moment, June addressed the fiend standing to his right.

"What you got, Unc?" asked June.

For the first time, June looked at the man and something in this fiend's eyes made him uncomfortable. He brushed it off as paranoia. He made a quick assessment, noticing the man's nappy skully, dingy dreadlocks, filthy clothes, along with the lint in his beard. He pegged him as harmless. June became irritated by the fiend's slow response and became disrespectful.

"Nigga! You fucking hard of hearing or what? What the fuck you want, Unc?" June yelled.

"I'll take a bundle." the fiend said through clenched teeth.

Hearing the fiend place a bundle order subsided June's tension. As he began retrieving the dope the fiend reached inside his army jacket and pulled out a huge, chrome, .50 caliber Desert Eagle. The sun glared off the shiny chrome causing a piercing light to reflect from the barrel. It caught June's attention from his peripheral vision. When he looked up to identify the light source, he was staring into the biggest barrel he had ever seen on a handgun. He heard the hammer cocking to his left. It was the other dreadhead fiend with a .357 aimed at his head. June raised his hands in submission.

"Take it all! You can have all the money. I got more drugs in the house." he stammered.

"We ain't come for no money or drugs! We soul snatchers, nigga! We came for ya life!" said one of the fiends.

Both guns fired simultaneously, knocking out the corners of June's head. The entire top half of his head was dismantled. A few more shots were pumped into his body for good measure before fleeing the scene in a silver Audi A6. Once the Audi was safely away from the scene, the passenger pulled off his dreadlock wig. He flipped down the visor mirror and slowly removed the fake beard.

"Drop us off at the other car and get rid of all this evidence." Psycho ordered Stickman.

Psycho was feeling alive after the murder that he and Taliban had committed. He was sorry to have lost his comrades, but he was happy to have the opportunity to unleash the war general trapped inside of him. Everyone involved in Moose and Pitbulls killing would pay... *He would make sure of it.*

Stickman was trusted with the task of getting rid of everything incriminating, including wigs, beards, clothes *and* the Audi. *Everything* was to be burned.

Chapter 15

Body was sitting in the Squirrel Hill home that he purchased for his mother and sister. He looked around at the interior of the home and felt a sense of pride in his ability to make such a grand purchase. Since he was a boy, he dreamt of accomplishing such feats. However, his pride quickly vanished and was replaced by feelings of embarrassment and shame. The shameful feelings stemmed from the source of Body's fortune, *heroin distribution*. Although he had his own opinion about street life, Body had been experiencing a discomfort that was attached to his participation in the drug game. He believed it was due largely in part to the upbringing and the core values he inherited from Mama Jones. Those values had Body straddling the fence, whether to continue in the drug game or depart from it once and for all. It was the upbringing which brought Body here to the house to have a much needed discussion with Robin, once more.

After the altercation between Body and Mama Jones, he had been carrying a heavy burden of guilt. Since then, he had a few conversations with his mother about getting clean and getting her life back on track. First and foremost for herself, then for her family who loved her tremendously. Years ago, Body attempted to have such conversations with Robin, but his attempts were met with hostility. He could remember times she slapped his face for what she called "not knowing his place". Nowadays, Robin seemed more receptive to the idea of treatment. Nobody can force an addict into recovery before they're ready. Body knew that. He was hoping that she would be ready sooner rather than later.

Robin came down the stairs and immediately embraced Body in a big hug.

"Jay Jay! Hey baby. I didn't know you were coming." said Robin. She was still the only person in the world who called him Jay Jay.

"Hey mom, you look good." Body said as he kissed her on the cheek. "Come on let's sit down. We should talk."

As mother and son sat in the living room on the couch, Body began, "I got some things on my mind and they've been bothering me a lot lately. We've had this conversation before, but it's time to take things more seriously and get proactive. You've told me on previous occasions that you want to get clean and I think that it's time."

"I agree, baby. It's been weighing heavily on my mind and I've been trying to decide the best time to do it and what to do about Jasmine." said Robin.

"Mom, with all due respect, Jas is aware of your problem. I can handle Jasmine's well being. I've been doing it all her life. You need to make a decision and you need to stick to it. What's it gonna be? Are you going to let us help you?"

"Yes, baby, I want help. I need help".

Robin had a floodgate of tears streaming down her face. Body embraced his mother with a hug. He knew it was his responsibility to take care of his women. He couldn't neglect the one who had given him life, no matter her flaws.

"We're gonna get you some help, Ma. As long as you want it for yourself. You'll be successful. But, there's one other thing, I want to discuss with you, Ma."

"What is it?" asked Robin. She lifted her head from Body's shoulder and looked at him through teary eyes.

"Listen Mom, I know all about your conception. Me and Grams have discussed it on a few occasions. You know how she is about history. She wanted me to know my own history, first and foremost." said Body.

"Why I have this light skin complexion and where it came from?"

Tears flowed down Robin's face as her baby boy revealed one of her dark secrets. There was one more deep dark secret that Robin harbored that she still wasn't ready to confront. She figured when the time was right, she would lay everything on the table. Body felt that he was a grown man and there was no better time than the present.

"I know what happened to grandma, and I can only imagine how you feel as a result of that. We all feel that pain, including me and Jas. We're a product of that as well because we're products of you. I'm bringing this up Ma because I think you should attend counseling, too, in addition to the substance abuse treatment. This is something we need to overcome as a family." said Body.

"Okay baby, I'll do it. I'll go to a treatment center. I'll attend NA meetings and I'll go to therapy. I'll do whatever it takes to be better. If it means being a better mother to you and Jas. I'll do anything. Come on, baby." She took Body by the hand. "Pray with me."

Body obliged. He knelt in front of the couch and prayed with his mother.

When he finished praying, Body was content with the progress he made with his raise. After he was finished speaking with Robin, he drove straight to the North Side to have another sit down with his grandraise. They talked for the better half of an hour and Body did something he hadn't done since he was a child. He cried. He shared with Mama Jones some of his recent tribulations, including his shame. And even though Mama Jones had been so angry and disappointed with Body, her maternal instincts kicked in and she consoled her grandson the way she used to when he was just a boy.

Together they made plans to enroll Robin in the best treatment facility in the city and to seek out a therapist who was best suited to handle situations similar to Robin's and their family. Mama Jones was proud of Body's recent sense of responsibility. She was happy that he was experiencing the kind of epiphanies that were causing some of his views to change. She could see a shift in his attitude and she was hoping that this shift was strong enough to save his life or that it would become stronger before it was too late.

She knew the potential that Body possessed. She was just waiting for him to realize it for himself. That day, she felt like it was the first step towards a new beginning.

When Body left Mama Jones's house, he breathed a huge sense of relief. An enormous amount of weight had been removed from his shoulders. Having those conversations with two of the people who meant the most to him in the entire world really helped. It was therapeutic in a sense. As he started his Range Rover, he felt a surge of energy. He pressed disc seven on his CD changer and used his remote to turn up the volume.

The sound of Omega's voice came blaring through the speakers:

"Chambonean sus armas para matarme aniquilarme ehh ehh, al tenerme de frente no son tan hombre para tirarme no ohh, me visto infrarrojo sobre mi cuerpo y colocado ehh ehh, y para dispararme no se' porque tiemblan tus manos"

Body loved to listen to a variety of music. It was easy to tell when he was in a good mood because he would play Spanish music. Most people would often mistake him for being Puerto Rican or maybe Dominican because of the features created by his mixed heritage and his ability to speak Spanish so well. The disc he was listening to was a mixed album that Mila put together for him. It was comprised of a variety of different artists and styles of music ranging from *Mambo* and *Romantica* to *Reggaeton* and *Bachata*. Once the song ended a popular tune called "Obsession" began. It was a song by Mila's favorite group, Aventura.

It made him think of her as he sang along to the lyrics, *"Son las cinco de la mañana y yo no he dormido nada, pensando en tu belleza, loco voy a parar..."*

Initially, Body planned to meet up with Psycho, but his unceasing thoughts of Mila caused him to detour and go home instead. When Body arrived, she was in the kitchen washing dishes, wearing a pair of fire engine red spandex shorts that exposed a hint of her ass cheeks and a black Victoria Secret bra. Body just stood in the entrance of the kitchen and watched her for a minute, admiring the sexiness of her body. Mila turned around and was slightly startled by Body's presence.

"Damn you scared me, Papi!" she said as she feigned fear by placing her right hand over her heart.

"How long you been standing there?" she asked in her sexy accent.

"Long enough to see everything I needed to see." he said with a smile.

"You stupid boy! Stop playing. I need to talk to you about something."

"¿Qué está en tu mente, Mami?"[20] asked Body.

He pulled her close, wrapped his arms around her waist and kissed her on the forehead. Mila snuggled into his arms and wrapped her arms around his waist.

She looked upwards into his eyes, "Estoy embarazada, Papi."[21]

The news caught Body totally by surprise, but the excitement was evident in his huge smile. He was cheesing from ear to ear.

"You mean, I'm about to be a father?"

"Yeah Papi, you happy?"

"Happy? I'm fucking ecstatic!"

He scooped Mila into his arms and kissed her passionately. She wrapped her thick legs around his waist and returned his passion. Body carried her over to the center of the kitchen and sat her atop of the

---

[20] What's on your mind mami?

[21] I'm pregnant, Papi.

island. He grabbed a handful of hair and tugged her head backward as he alternated between intense acts of foreplay, nibbling on her chin, licking her neckline and kissing her clavicle. Body knew what drove her wild. He cupped a handful of her breasts and squeezed. Then, he unfastened her bra which was clasped together in the front. Her melon sized breast sat firmly, enticing him, and her nipples stood erect as he gently brushed over them with the print of his thumbs. He used the pointer finger and thumb to squeeze her nipples. Soft moans of pleasure escaped her lips as Body took his time, teasing her and building her up. He eased his fingers in the elastic waistband of her spandex shorts and began to peel them off of her. She lifted her legs in an upward angle and made it easier to pull the shorts completely off. He grasped her legs behind the knees and kept them elevated as he buried his face in her lap of love. It drove her absolutely crazy the way he would eat her pussy. He never failed to send her body into convulsions. He picked her up off the island and carried her to the bedroom where he delicately stroked her with a precision she felt only *he* could provide. They made love until exhaustion. The sheets were damp with sweat and Mila's back was sticking to Body's chest. He gently stroked her hair as they conversed.

"Damn, I gotta get my shit together, Baby. You know how important it is to me to be a good father. Shit, an excellent father."

"You will be, Papi. Don't worry."

"I can't help but worry. This shit is serious. What if I'm not good enough?"

"Don't talk like that. Papi, you're gonna do just fine."

"I hope so, Mami. I hope so."

***

While Body was concerned with parenthood and the functionality of his family, Psycho was focused on who needed to be spanked to guarantee their success. He had huge ambitions when it came to the drug game. If he were able to keep those same ambitions and change his aspirations, he could have been an executive of a Fortune 500 Company. But instead, he aspired to be the biggest kingpin the "Steel City" had ever seen.

He was well on his way to obtaining his goals. He had managed to spread his wings and was supplying half of the heroin entering the city. But what he really wanted was to supply 100% of all the *drugs* entering the city. He dreamed of operating outside his city and state. But before he would be able to enforce a reign elsewhere, Psycho first had to handle the situation brewing in his own backyard. The conflict with Marv' and his crew had gone on far too long for his liking.

Nearly a year passed since things escalated between the opposing crews. Every time Psycho recruited new workers for Centre Ave, they would be shot or killed. Vice versa was true about the opposition. Anytime Marv' attempted to regain control of the avenue, he was quickly met with vicious maneuvers from Psycho. He nor Marv' needed Centre Ave in order to thrive but, each man's pride forbade him to yield to the opposition. Psycho reflected back to a conversation he had with Body a short while back. Body told him that Centre Ave may not be worth all the trouble it was sure to bring. In hindsight, Psycho silently agreed with Body's viewpoint, but the situation was well beyond reconciliation and he was well aware that the streets were watching. He planned to end the feud as soon as possible but it proved to be difficult. Marvin was very elusive and had extensive resources.

Marvin had been around for a long time and had built quite a few relationships. His most important relationships were those he had built with a crew of shooters to handle any problems that may arise, like the one he found himself involved in with Body and Psycho. He had long ago left behind the days when he had to be seen on the streets to conduct business. Factored in with all of the money he had managed to accumulate, it was easy for him to make things happen from behind the scenes and stay out of the crosshairs of Psycho's gun.

Psycho believed that it would be a lot easier to get 2-Gunz out of the way. He worried the move would possibly drive Marv' further into hiding. Even though his disdain for 2-Gunz had continued to grow over time and he would love nothing more than to bring him to his knees. He could hear Body's voice in his head "strike the shepherd and the sheep will scatter." That was a law that he picked up from the 48 Laws of Power, which happened to be Body's favorite book. Psycho had become very fond of the book as well. It laid out the laws in which they lived by. At times, Psycho may have needed a reminder. Body had no problem reminding him. Ever since they were children, Body had been the voice of reason for Psycho, who was hot headed and quick tempered. Psycho didn't need any reminders of one thing though. It was better to end a war or a fight as soon as possible. The more it dragged on, the more danger you were exposed to. That's why the war with Marvin and 2-Gunz was really bothering him. He wanted it over with and he had a different way of handling the situation this time. He decided to share his strategy with Body to get his closest comrade's input.

Chapter 16

Buzz Buzz Buzz

Body looked at the nightstand when he heard his cell phone vibrating. He reached over to pick up the phone and looked at the caller ID to screen the call before answering. He recognized Psycho's number and answered immediately.

"What's up, Psych?" Body greeted.

"Aint shit. Got a few things I need to run pass you. Where you at?"

"I'm at the crib with wifey. Swing through."

"Aight. I'm near Homewood right now. So, I'll be there in a few minutes."

"Aight, I'll be here."

"Bet."

With that, Psycho closed his cell phone and drove up Frankstown Avenue in route to Penn Hills. It took him less than 15 minutes to arrive. He pulled into the driveway behind Mila's white 645 convertible BMW. Body saw his headlights as he pulled into the driveway and met him at the door. Psycho entered the house and sat in the living room.

"I'm 'bout to grab a Pepsi. You want something to drink?" offered Body.

"Yeah, let me get one, too."

Body went into the kitchen to get the two Pepsi's from the fridge. Psycho made his way over to the mini bar. He grabbed two glasses and the gallon of Hennessy that was half empty. He poured shots for them as Body returned with the Pepsi. He passed the Pepsi to Psycho who declined.

"I'm good now. Imma fuck with this Henny." Psycho liked to drink his Hennessy straight, whereas Body couldn't tolerate the strong taste and always needed a chaser.

"So, what's on ya mind?" asked Body.

"It's like this. The beef with Gunz and them niggas has been going on too long. It's time to put an end to this shit, once and for all. It's not a good look letting this shit keep dragging along. I know we've already talked about the whole *strike the shepherd and the sheep will scatter* thing. We both know that Marv' is at the top of this thing pulling all the strings. But, what I think is more important is, the fact that Gunz is at the top of his army. Right now Marv' is breaking one the cardinal rules of the 48 Laws of Power. He's building himself behind a fortress which separates him from what's really happening in these streets. The only connection he has to what's going on out here is Gunz. If he's not the only one, he's *definitely* the primary one. Other than that, there's the nigga Livewire. I already got the drop on that little dirty nigga. I can bake his ass a cake, easily. I'm ready to put that in motion asap. But, as far as that nigga Gunz is concerned. I think if we get *him* out of the way, then we cut the legs from under that nigga Marv.'" said Psych.

"That shit makes sense. We can neutralize his power with a move like that." Body agreed.

"Hell yeah, we can. Me and Taliban gonna get on top of that shit asap." said Psycho.

"Aight, but while you're thinking about that. I got some shit lined up for us that has huge potential." said Body.

"Oh yeah? What's good?"

"Remember, we were talking 'bout getting back into the coke game? If we can get a connect with the right number?"

"Yeah." said Psycho.

"Well, I hollered at Carlito to see if he knew anything good. It turns out, he can get his hands on that shit. He spoke to his pop's over in Columbia and he's willing to plug us in. But he wants to meet face to face, first. I already told 'Lito that I have a partner. So, he knows all about you. He told me that the stakes go up fucking with the coke game."

"Why would the stakes go up with the coke, when keys of dope cost more? That don't make sense." said Psych.

"It's like this. Them niggas send birds of dope for distribution, but the coke comes more in abundance. So basically, they ain't fucking with no small time niggas with that shit. They looking for a nigga to cop 100 birds or more."

"Damn!" said Psycho.

"Right now, them shits are still going for $35,000 to $36,000 for a single one. We should be able to get those shits for at least $20,000. We just gotta meet the nigga and negotiate the number." said Body.

"Aight. When do we meet him?"

"We meet him in a couple days. I'll be getting all the flight info together in the meantime."

"Why you need flight info? We gonna fly to Jersey?" asked Psycho.

"Nahh, my nigga. We flying to Medellin."

***

Two days later, Body and Psycho were dropped off by Stickman at Pittsburgh International Airport. They each had a single travel bag slung over their shoulders. They didn't plan to stay long, so they packed very light. They didn't have to check any bags because their bags met carry-on requirements. Their flight was scheduled for departure at 8:45 am. They arrived early to ensure they wouldn't run into any problems that would affect their flight. Body and Psycho still had a half-hour before boarding, so they went to Auntie Anne's pretzel shop for a few cinnamon and sugar pretzels.

After seemingly forever, flight 217 was called to board. Body and Psycho grabbed their bags and headed for the plane where they sat first class.

After the plane had taken off, Body got the attention of the stewardess and ordered a shot to calm his nerves. Anytime he was on an airplane, he felt tension. He enjoyed a shot of vodka to put his nerves at ease. After he drank his shot, Body laid his head against the shaded window and slept. Psycho was doing the same in the aisle in front of him.

At 11:45 am, they were awakened by the landing of the plane at Miami International Airport where they had an hour layover before heading to Columbia. They went over to Chick-fil-A and bought a couple of chicken sandwiches and Sprites while they waited for their next flight. They sat at a nearby table and enjoyed their lunch.

"Yo, ever since you told me about this move, I couldn't sleep. Even on the plane, I tried to relax, but I couldn't sleep. I keep thinking about how I don't wanna fuck this move up." said Psycho.

"You won't fuck it up, nigga. You a hustler." said Body.

"Yeah, but a hundred keys?"

Psycho suddenly leaned closer to Body and began to whisper as if someone may be listening.

"A hundred keys is a lot of work, my nigga."

"I know we can move them." said Body.

"Yeah, but how fast? We haven't been dealing with this shit in a minute. It might take a while to get shit flowing." said Psycho.

"Well, the way I see it is. If we can negotiate the right price, no one will even come close as far as competition goes. We already know the niggas in the city that sell birds. We'll be in a position to serve them niggas. So, we'll get rid of most of them shits through wholesale. Other than that, I figure we should open up shop on Bentley, again." said Body.

"I was thinking that, too. I got some niggas I can put down there. I got some lil cousins over in Homewood, straight wild cowboys. Them niggas are official. Let's bring them in. We can feed 'em. Like you said, we should be getting the right price that will put us in a position to make sure nobody can compete with us down there. We can move a bird a day, easily. Plus, we can put Menace down there too in a different apartment to sell weight to niggas who want ounces and shit. That should cover at least another half a bird or whole." said Psycho.

"Yeah, I think it will cover a bird or more because we'll have cheaper ounces than anybody else. But the distribution has to change as far as the hand to hand business goes." responded Body.

"What you mean?" asked Psycho.

"I mean, we need a way to keep track of all the money that comes through the block. Of course, we'll put one of our people down there we can trust. But I don't think we should have niggas dipping." said Body.

Dipping was Pittsburgh slang for selling crack that wasn't packaged.

"So, what you wanna do? You wanna have that shit bagged up?" asked Psycho.

"Nah, not bagged up, bottled up. It's a new marketing strategy for the city." Body said in between bites of his chicken sandwich.

"I've never seen bottles around." replied Psycho.

"Me neither, that's some New York shit. So I figure, a move like that could potentially be big for us. Shit, niggas always looking for something new, even with this dope game. They want white bags now, *instead of blue.* They like black stamps, *instead of red.* It's all psychological. Ain't like the dope changed because the bag did. It's just marketing. It's the business. Now, we can market this crack differently too, just like the dope game. We'll use bottles and sell half grizzys for $20 a pop. We can calculate everything from there. If this coke is right how that nigga say it is, we'll bring back an extra half of *melt*. That's mad extra ounces from every cook up. At $40 a gram, we're looking at a lil over $60,000 a chic' give or take." said Body.

"Sounds official, but where do we get those bottles from?" asked Psycho.

"I know a spot in Jersey. I can place an order and get them shits in bulk. I already been doing homework on it. They got some shit called LL40 that can hold a half gram. There's the LL25 for the dimes and SS25 for the nicks. Every bottle will be filled to maximum capacity with no shaking room." said Body.

"Aight, let's try it. Reminds me of some *New Jack City* shit." Psycho laughed.

As they conversed and finished their lunch, they heard the lady make the announcement over the intercom, *"Flight 813 now boarding. Flight 813 now boarding."*

They grabbed their carry-ons and hurried to the terminal. Once again, they were seated in first class. Body had his traditional shot after take off. A few hours and a half-dozen shots later, they were landing in Medellin, Colombia. They gathered their bags from the overhead compartments and exited the plane.

As they made their way through the airport, they were approached by a man wearing a light gray designer suit, white shirt, and no tie.

"Tu eres Body, verdad?"[22]

---

[22] You're Body, right?

"Si!"[23] responded Body and accepted the handshake.

"Placer conocerte. Mi nombre es Juan!"[24] said the man revealing his identity, delivered with a smile.

"You must be Psycho." he said, extending the same pleasantry.

"I work for Mr. Valencia. Please follow me." Juan began to navigate his way through the crowded airport with Body and Psycho in tow. They made eye contact and gave each other knowing looks. No words were necessary. They realized the power of the people they were dealing with by their subtle approach. The way the man already knew who they were *and* could differentiate the two . Yet, they had no clue who he was at the time. They had never heard of him.

They exited through the automated glass doors and stepped into 96 degree Columbian heat. Once outside, they were approached by a different man wearing a black suit with a white shirt underneath. The four men who flanked him were similarly dressed, two on the left and two on the right.

"This is Eduardo." said Juan, introducing Body and Psycho to the short, stocky cowboy.

The men exchanged handshakes. Then, Eduardo took their bags and showed them to their awaiting vehicle. As Eduardo reached for the bags, Body noticed the MP5 submachine gun inside of his suit jacket. They hopped into a white Suzuki jeep that was wedged between two white Mitsubishi jeeps. There were two men waiting outside each Mitsubishi jeep dressed casually in jeans and blazers. Body and Psycho

---

[23] Yes!

[24] Pleased to meet you. My name is Juan.

got into the rear of the Suzuki. Juan was in the passenger seat and Eduardo drove. The rest of the men piled into the Mitsubishis. They all pulled away from the curb, one after the other.

Psycho and Body took in the scenery on the drive to the Valencia estate. Juan informed them that they would be staying at the estate for the duration of their time in Columbia. Any mention of staying at a hotel was a preposterous idea. The drive to the estate was nearly two and a half hours. They drove on off-road terrain and into the jungle for forty-five minutes, before pulling up to the ranch style estate. They pulled up to the gate where a half-dozen men stood brandishing machine guns. They briefly stopped at the gate waiting for clearance and were given entry.

Body and Psycho were in awe of the size and layout of the estate. Nestled on forty sprawling acres of green pastures, it accommodated a stable of three dozen thoroughbred horses. Armed guards patrolled the property on horsebacks, four-wheelers or dune buggies. There was a helicopter landing pad a few yards away from a landing strip. The strip led to a hanger that housed a G4 jet and an assortment of single and double engine Cessnas.

The inside of the mansion was just as magnificent with ten bedrooms, twelve bathrooms, two kitchens, indoor and outdoor swimming pools, a sauna, a jacuzzi, an in-home theater and a state of the art gym. The two were impressed, to say the least. They had only seen similar homes on *MTV Cribs* or some other show , which highlighted the life of the rich and famous.

Juan led them through the corridors of the house out onto a huge terrace where Mr. Valencia was enjoying brunch. Juan approached him and whispered something in his ear. Mr. Valencia looked toward Body and Psycho then stood to his feet to greet the men hospitably.

"¿Cómo están amigos?"[25] said Mr. Valencia, offering up handshakes.

Body shook his hand first.

"Estoy bien, gracias.[26] I'm Body and this is my partner, Psycho."

"Yes, yes good to meet you both. I've heard a lot of good things about you boys. Come, let's sit." said Mr. Valencia.

They sat at a table near the edge of the terrace overlooking an enormous backyard equipped with a jacuzzi, an olympic size swimming pool, a basketball court, a tennis court and a soccer field. Mr. Valencia was a huge fan of what he called *football or futbol*. It was rumored that he owned a professional team.

There were more than a dozen scantily clad women milling around the pool, simply sunbathing and sipping their colorful drinks. Some of the girls were topless. All of them were beautiful. They all looked like supermodels or video vixens. Body and Psycho found it a little difficult to concentrate on the task at hand with such beautiful women in close proximity. Being at the strip club was one thing, but this was different. This was *Playboy Mansion* shit. Body knew he had to be careful with his wandering eyes because of his relationship with Mr. Valencia's daughter. He knew it would be disrespectful to lust in front

---

[25] How are you, my friends?

[26] I'm well, thank you.

of Mila's father, so he forced himself to focus on the business he had flown all the way to Columbia to handle.

Mr. Valencia was going down memory lane. He talked about how he first got started in the business and even about his childhood. How he wasn't from Medellin. Instead, he was born in Bogota`, Colombia, the neighborhood of Barranquilla.

He told stories about all of the beautiful women there, including the famous singer Shakira and actress Sofia Vergara. He painted pictures of women as beautiful as the famed singer and actress being used as mules to transport drugs. He explained how models used their visas for easy access into the states and would take with them pounds of cocaine and heroin. The girls were sent not only from Columbia, but the neighboring countries as well, including Venezuela and Aruba.

They learned that he had been involved in the drug trade since he was a boy. Mr. Valencia discussed how he started out as a runner and eventually worked himself up the ladder to a high position in the North Coast Cartel. He explained how he was responsible for the havoc wreaked on Barranquilla in the early 1990's, by pushing aside any competition. After static began to build between him and the top bosses of the North Coast Cartel, he disappeared and severed ties completely. After the death of Pablo Escobar, Medellin belonged to whoever was strong enough to take it. Eventually, Mr. Valencia found himself in Medellin, where he started his own business and built an army strong enough to take the North Coast Cartel head on. He was once the general of their army. He knew exactly what to expect from them. This kind of knowledge allowed him to thwart all efforts and squash them in war. He told tales of destroying his enemies as Juan chimed in with affirmations. He told them how he located his enemies and their families and went so far as to discuss the disposal of bodies. The stories were gruesome, to say the least. Now, he runs a very lucrative operation from Medellin.

Chapter 17

Psycho was no slouch when it came to the murder game, but even he had to admit that these niggas were on some other shit. He recognized all the threatening subtleties in their stories and the underlying tone in Juan's voice, which made him uneasy. Psycho didn't do well with being threatened, but he was no fool. He planned to make it back to America in one piece. Plus, he respected the moral of the story, "Don't you ever fuck me over." The message was very clear.

After they were finished telling their stories, Mr. Valencia was ready to get down to business. He explained to Body and Psycho all of his expectations relating to their partnership.

"I'm looking for consistency. Someone who I can build a relationship with that will stand the test of time. Loyalty is a priceless commodity in this business. I expect yours and you'll certainly have mine." said Mr. Valencia.

"You have mine, too." said Body.

"Good, good." said Mr. Valencia.

They were engrossed in their own conversation as Psycho and Juan looked on.

"I'm looking for a commitment from you as a business partner of mine, Body."

"What kind of commitment are you looking for, Mr. Valencia?

"Enough of the formalities, Amigo. Call me Jesus." said Mr. Valencia.

"Ok, Jesus. What kind of commitment are you looking for from your business partners?"

"Well for starters, I need to be the sole supplier. Additionally, I'm looking for a commitment of 150 kilos per month."

Body felt a lump in his throat, but managed to maintain his composure. A hundred and fifty kilos was fifty more than he was prepared to commit to. He still wasn't completely convinced that he could get rid of a hundred kilos. But this wasn't an opportunity, he was willing to pass up. So, he maintained his poker face.

"That's interesting. 150 kilos is a lot of blow. I'm sure you would agree?" Body said, maintaining his eye contact.

"Just like you, I'm also looking for a commitment from my business partner."

Jesus lit a cigar. He took a pull and studied Body inquisitively. Body continued while he still had the momentum.

"I'm looking for a commitment to steady pricing and pure product. For a commitment like 150 kilos per month, I need my number at $15,000 a piece." His brazen negotiation caused Jesus to chuckle.

"You're very ambitious, parcero[27]. But, no way can I do $15,000. My cocaine is pure and I'm taking all of the risks. I guarantee it's quality and pay for safe delivery. When you can share some of the

---

[27] Partner

risks, then you have the leverage to make such requests. Entiendes?[28]
So, for now, the price will be $28,000." said Jesus.

Body shook his head as a negative.

"That won't work. That's a $4,200,000 price tag. I'm just beginning to wet my feet with this. But, my network has huge potential and 150 kilos just won't due in a very short while. I'm an investment, Jesus. No different than buying stock in *Microsoft* or some other top Fortune 500 company. I guarantee a return on your investment. And I'm willing to share the risks associated with my shipments. As long as I can have creative input on transportation strategies." said Body.

"I can appreciate your aspirations, amigo. But, this is what I'm willing to do. You will share in some of the risks by picking up your shipment in Florida. In return, you will pay $3.45 million. That's $23,000 per kilo, and a $750,000 difference. That's the best I can do."

"Sounds like a deal." said Body.

"Good. The first shipment is on me. By the time you reach the states, 150 kilos will be waiting on you." said Jesus.

He liked the vibe he got from Body and Psycho almost immediately and arranged for a dozen girls to fly out of Ezeiza International Airport in Buenos Aires, Argentina.

"After this shipment, you have to pick it up in Miami. This one will be delivered to Pittsburgh." said Jesus.

That was music to Body and Psycho's ears. It was hard for either of them to sit still knowing that there was 150 kilos just waiting for distribution.

---

[28] Understand?

After they wrapped up their business dealings, everyone retired inside the mansion to the lounge area. Jesus turned on the 82" TV to watch the soccer game between Mexico and Argentina. Jesus ordered a servant to prepare a meal to accommodate his guests.

Although Psycho hadn't eaten anything in the past few hours, the only thing he was thinking about eating was one of the vixens lounging poolside. He excused himself from the company of the men and made his way outside where the women were. Psycho walked through the terrace and stood near the edge of the pool watching the ladies for a second. He was trying to decide which one he liked most.

All of the women possessed an exotic beauty with complexions ranging from milky white to fudge. One girl, in particular, caught Psycho's eye. Her complexion was milk chocolate and she stood erect at 5'2". Her legs were thick and symmetric to her fat ass. She reminded Psycho of the vixen, Ki-toy. She had washboard abs and small perky titties. He guessed a B-cup.

He walked over to her as she exited the pool. She had on a yellow bikini. The swimming cap on her head was bunched up at the top, which gave Psycho the impression she either had long hair or hella weave. He guessed weave. She looked up at Psycho and watched him as he approached her.

Suddenly, he was standing directly in front of her. He looked down at her and took the time to admire her full lips covered in gloss and her big pretty brown eyes. She stood there with her hand on her hip in reverse fashion and matched his gaze in a defiant manner.

"You gonna say something or you just gonna stand there and stare?" she said in her thick Colombian accent.

Psycho was taken aback by her forwardness and the fact that she spoke English. Her sassiness was sexiness for Psycho. He was turned on.

"Yeah. I'm gonna say something. I was just caught up in ya beauty. That's all. Plus, I wasn't quite sure what to say. I don't speak Spanish. All I know is '*Como estas and gracias*'. That shit wouldn't have gotten me anywhere. I would've had to get an interpreter. I'm Psycho, by the way." he said and went for the handshake.

"Psycho? What kind of name is that? I know your mother didn't name you Psycho?"

"No, my real name is Raymond, but don't tell anybody." he replied with a smile.

"Raymond? I like that. Placer conocerte, Raymond. That means, it's a pleasure to meet you." she said.

"Oh, you gonna teach me Spanish?" he replied amused.

"Maybe," she replied with a playful wink. "I'm Claudia." she said as she pulled off her swimming cap revealing a head full of perfectly manicured dreadlocks hanging below her shoulders. Somehow, this added to her beauty and gave her more of an exotic look.

She smiled at Psycho exposing a perfect set of pearly white teeth. He was feeling a bit mesmerized by this girl and didn't know why.

"Claudia, huh? I like that. I never knew there were girls like you in Colombia or I would've made this trip a long time ago."

"Girls like me? There are *no* girls like me in Colombia."

"Well, you don't look like most Latinas. I mean, I don't wanna sound stereotypical. It's just that you look like a sista." Psycho responded.

"A sister?" she asked.

"Yeah, you know, a sista, a Black woman?" said Psycho.

"Oh," she said as she laughed. "Una morena." said Claudia.

"Say what?" asked Psycho.

"In Spanish, we say *morena*. I'm a morena because of my darker complexion. You need to get out more. You'll see that *we* come in all different shades. *We* have African ancestry, too. So, we come a lot darker than *this*." said Claudia.

"I guess you really do have some things to teach me." said Psycho. "Teach me some things about ya self."

"What do you wanna know?" she asked.

"What do you do?" asked Psycho.

"I'm a business woman, an entrepreneur."

Psycho and Claudia conversed for what seemed like forever. He learned that she worked for Jesus, which immediately drew a red flag. But, it was quickly clarified that her line of work wasn't prostitution. Although, exactly what she did was never specified. Psycho assumed she was one of those model type mules that Jesus had mentioned earlier. He learned that she had been to the states a few times, but it was always business. That information further solidified his theory of her being in the trafficking business.

Psycho tried hard to push up on Claudia. He tried to get her to spend the night with him, but she declined. Instead, they exchanged information and promised to stay in touch with one another. Psycho extended an invitation to Claudia to visit him in the states. He expressed to her that not only did he want to, but he *needed* to see her again. Psycho was surprised by his own statement. He was always running game to one girl or another, so it wasn't the fact that he had said these things. It was the fact that he actually *meant* it.

Body and Psycho spent the night at Jesus' estate. They awoke bright and early the next morning for their flight back to the states. They didn't have anything to pack, so they quickly showered, brushed their teeth and were ready to hit the road. As they descended the stairs, they were approached by one of the maids. She escorted them to the dining area, where the chef had prepared a hearty breakfast. They sat at the table and enjoyed breakfast with Jesus. A few things were reiterated to ensure everyone was on the same page.

After breakfast, Eduardo took their bags and loaded them in the SUV. They wrapped things up with Jesus and were on their way. As when they arrived, they rode back to the airport in a caravan of SUVs with Eduardo and Juan.

By 9:45 am, they were nestled in the leather of their first class seats. By 12:15 am, they were back in Miami for a 45 minute layover. On the flight back to Pittsburgh, all Psycho could think of was Claudia. While Body was trying to figure out how to get rid of one hundred and fifty kilos and how the hell he was gonna move shipments out of Miami of all places. That interstate was hotter than the Mexican border. He knew it would be extremely dangerous to try moving that many kilos out of that city or state. But all of a sudden, he developed an ingenious idea. He turned to share his thoughts with Psycho, but he was already fast asleep.

When they arrived back in Pittsburgh, Taliban and Stickman were waiting. Body called them when they landed in Miami and gave them the scheduled arrival time. Stickman was circling the airport in the black Dodge Durango. After the 9/11 attack, no one could park in front of the airport or sit idly waiting for a traveler. By the 3rd lap, Body and Psycho were waiting curbside. They jumped in the truck and greeted their boys. They happily shared the good news from their trip.

"Damn! 150 keys? Fuck we supposed to do with all that work?" asked Taliban.

"We *supposed* to sell it, nigga." Psycho said with more confidence than he felt.

"Man, it's gonna take three years to sell all that shit." said Stickman laughing.

"Nah, we just gotta get shit slapping. We'll get rid of that shit in no time. My people from Jersey sent somebody through here, right?" asked Body.

"Yeah. The nigga came through with hell of boxes. They wasn't heavy though, but I didn't open them. I just put them in the spot." replied Stickman.

"That's cool. 'Cause that's exactly where we need them at. We 'bout to try something new. But first, I gotta get to the library." said Body.

"The library? What you need at the library?" Stickman asked.

"I need to use the computer. That's what I use to communicate with the plug. I'm about to do the same thing for my people in Jersey and our major customers here in the city. The dope game is going viral, my nigga." Body said laughing.

"That's some smart shit." said Taliban.

"Aight. I'm gonna go to the Martin Luther King Library on Centre Ave. As a matter of fact, Stick, go to Oakland. I'm gonna use the computers in the Pitt University Building."

When they arrived in Oakland, Body and Psycho exited the truck and went into the building, blending right in with dozens of college students. They found an unoccupied computer in the back. Body turned on the computer and logged in using a friend of Mila's student account to communicate with the connect. When he logged in, there was a message waiting for him. It was short and concise:

Red Roof Inn. Robinson Township. Room 203.

After reading the message, he logged off. He and Psycho exited the library and got back into the truck.

"So, what's good?" asked Stickman.

"First, we gotta go get the Cherokee. It's in the parking garage over on Liberty. Then, we gotta hit Robinson Township. Everything is supposed to be waiting for us. The Cherokee has a stash box, so I want you to drive that Stick because you're the best driver." said Body.

"Taliban, you ride with him. We'll follow yall." said Psycho.

Taliban felt a twinge of jealousy after Body called Stickman the best driver. He knew Stickman was good, but he felt he could take him.

"You know where the Red Roof Inn is at, right?" Stickman nodded his head in agreement.

"Aight, that's where we're going." said Body.

Stickman pulled over in front of the parking garage and everybody exited the truck. Body climbed into the driver seat with Psycho riding shotgun. Taliban and Stickman loaded into the SRT8 Cherokee parked on the second level of the garage. They pulled out front and took the lead as Body followed behind them.

Chapter 18

It took twenty five minutes to reach Robinson Township. They parked on the opposite end of the motel's office to avoid unwanted attention. The two SUVs parked side by side. Body killed the engine and he and Psycho exited the vehicle.

"Stay here. We won't need ya'll on this one." said Body.

He and Psycho went to the stairwell and climbed to the second level in search of room 203. Once they found the room they knocked on the door. They could hear the shuffling of feet inside the room.

"Who's there?" said a woman's voice in a thick Spanish accent.

"Body!" he replied.

The woman opened the door and allowed the men to enter the room. Once inside, they looked around and noticed that there only appeared to be the three women present. They were as beautiful as Jesus described them to be. They weren't dressed glamorous, but their beauty was undeniable. Psycho was disappointed that Claudia wasn't one of the three women. It was just wishful thinking on his part. He was hoping the reason she couldn't or wouldn't spend the night with him was because she had to get on a plane to have the work there before his arrival.

"¿Cómo están, mujeres?"[29] said Body.

---

[29] How are you doing, ladies?

"¿Cómo está, Papi?"[30] replied the two girls with big smiles on their faces. Their flirtatious nature was apparent.

"We have everything ready to go." said the light- skinned girl, who answered the door.

Body never bothered to ask the girls their names because he just wanted to be in and out. He knew if they became any more friendly, his trips would become business *and* pleasure. One of the other girls rolled large size travel luggage from the closet. There were three in total, all equipped with wheels for easy transportation. Body quickly estimated that there were fifty kilos in each luggage. Psycho called Taliban on his cell phone and summoned him to the room. When he got there, he was given one of the bags which was seemingly a ton on his adolescent body. They said their goodbyes to the women and were out the door.

"I don't know what the fuck I was thinking. I knew we were picking up all this shit, but it never occurred to me how heavy this shit is. I wasn't even gonna act like I was gonna lug two of these big ass bags to the car. " said Body.

"I wonder how dem chicks got these shits in the room." Psycho retorted.

"Who are these chicks, anyway?" asked Taliban. "Them bitches fine as hell."

"Yeah, but this shit is strictly business, my nigga. Otherwise, I'd still be up there right now." said Psycho and they all laughed.

---

30 What's up, Papi?

They broke down the luggage and loaded it into the stash box of the Cherokee located on the floor underneath the backseat. At that moment they realized there was a problem. The secret compartment was built to hold a maximum of fifty kilos. They removed the kilos from the bag and laid them in the compartment. There were a hundred that couldn't fit.

"Fuck!" said Body, expressing his frustration.

"Look, just put the bags in the hatch. You gotta drive safe and follow the speed limit. We'll follow you. If shit gets hot, then we'll ram the pigs, so ya'll can get away. Ain't no way we're taking a loss on 150 birds." said Body.

"Aight. Bet." said Stickman.

They hoisted the remaining two bags into the hatch of the truck and hit the road. Twenty five minutes later, they reached the stash house without incident. They were using Mila's old house in Oakland to store the bulk of the work. They dropped off a hundred and forty kilos and took ten birds to the trap house to prepare for distribution.

When they arrived on Forbes Ave, Body and Psycho took the cocaine straight to the kitchen. They prepared to do work in a lab that could rival any chemist. They cooked one bird at a time. The first one came back over 1,600 grams. They knew they were dealing with official quality. The crack was sent into the other room to be bottled up. Stickman, Taliban, Man Man, and Menace all got to work asap. Body left the house to make a run while Psycho continued to cook up birds. Twenty minutes later, Body returned with containers of B12. Psycho knew exactly what his man was thinking, when he saw the containers.

They would cut the keys that were slated for wholesale distribution instead of selling it, so pure. They measured their recipe of B12 and mixed it with the proper ratio of cocaine. They used a spray bottle to moisten it in preparation to be compressed. If there was one thing they knew how to do, it was to stretch a buck.

Psycho got on the phone and called a few girls that he used to bag up dope. Now, he hired them to bottle crack. As soon as the first thousand vials were filled, Body had Psycho call up his family in Homewood. He was hoping they were as tough as Psycho led on because he would need someone *thorough* for the task at hand. He would give strict instructions to give all one thousand vials away free. They were samples to be used as a mere marketing ploy.

***

It didn't take long for the word to spread that *free* crack was being given away. It took less than a half-hour to pass out the vials. Body received the response he had hoped for. Everyone wanted to purchase the product. He left the young hustlers on Bentley with a promise to return shortly with something to sell. He went back to the traphouse to relay the news to everybody. Everyone was happy to hear the news.

Body pulled Menace to the side to discuss the plans he had in mind for him. Menace was happy to finally get some action outside of the bag-up table. Body gave him $30,000 worth of vials for the boys on Bentley. It would be his responsibility to make sure things were functioning properly as well as distribute weight to the projects. He was given fifty-six ounces of crack with instructions to sell them for $900 a piece. Most of the numbers in the city reflected around $1,300 per ounce. The move Body was orchestrating was certain to poach plenty of clientele. He secured an apartment in the projects for Menace to set up shop. He also provided him with a walkie-talkie to communicate with the runners, a police scanner to keep track of police movement and a list of frequencies to know which channels were law enforcement. The only thing he had to decide was who would be there with him to watch his back.

"I got somebody in mind to watch my back." said Menace.

"Aight, cool. One more thing, you gotta follow the rules. Only one person in the crib at a time to cop. And *no* discussing business on the phone." said Body.

"I got this, Bro. Don't worry." said Menace.

Body went to Bentley with Menace to make sure everything was set up right. Once he was comfortable with how everything looked, he headed home.

Chapter 19

Livewire was sitting in his mother's living room plotting his next come up. He was accompanied by his new partner in crime, Chubs. He got his nickname from his grandraise, when he was a baby because of his chubby cheeks and pudgy body. At fifteen years old he still maintained his baby fat, so the name suited him well.

Livewire recruited Chubs because he was young and impressionable. He looked up to him. Livewire used that to his advantage because Chubs was '*bout that action*! He quickly earned himself a reputation in the hood for robbing all the local convenience stores and gas stations. Livewire knew the job he had in mind was a two man job. So, he decided to bring Chubs. Usually, he would've been with Junior. But, after he was *spanked* Livewire had trouble replacing him. The good thing about Chubs was his youth. Livewire could mold him.

"Look, this is the deal. I got the drop on some nigga from Duquesne. His stupid ass like showing off for bitches and taking them to his house. My bitch was fucking with this nigga, when I was locked up and put me up on game. Some nigga they call Lex. She said he was fronting hard for her, telling her he got his name because he got the new drop top Lexus. And he got a presidential *Rolex* on the sleeve, mad corny shit. He took her to the crib while his girl and baby were gone on some sleazy shit. She knew he lived there with his girl and baby because she saw the family pictures on the nightstand that he tried to lay face down. Then the dumb ass nigga had the nerve to open his safe in front of her. She said it's behind the painting over top of the bed. She said she saw a lot of stacks in that shit. So, we gotta hit this lick tonight! Lisa is gonna hook up with this nigga, again, so we can get him how we want him. I already know where he lives. I drove past to scope it out, yesterday. All we gotta do now is wait." said Livewire.

"That's cool. I'm with that. I got this Millennium .9mm right here. So, I'm ready!" said Chubs.

Livewire could see that he was anxious.

"Yeah, you can take that .9mm with you as back up, but I want you to hold shit down with a shotty. I got a nice pump for you in the closet." said Livewire.

He went to retrieve the shotgun. Then, passed it to Chubs. Excitement registered in his eyes as he examined the double action shotgun in his hands.

"Yeah, this will work right here." said Chubs with a sinister smile on his face.

By 11:00pm Livewire's girlfriend, Lisa, was riding around with Lex in his new champagne SC 430 convertible Lexus.

"I'm hungry, Boo." Lisa told him.

"Aight, let's get something to eat. Where you wanna go?" asked Lex.

"I just want something real quick 'cause I got a headache right now. Let's go to Wendy's on the boulevard." she suggested.

That was just fine with Lex because it was a cheap meal. He still planned to fuck her, headache and all.

As Lex drove enroute of Baum Blvd, Lisa was busy texting:

We 'bout to go to Wendy's on the blvd. right now then I'll have him take me home. I told him that I have a headache. I know his whack ass still gonna try to fuck. I'll pretend to give in and hit you when I get there.

Lisa put her phone down and reclined her seat.

Livewire felt his cell phone buzz in his pocket. It was another text from Lisa. He knew there would be details needed for his upcoming lick. He silently read it to himself:

Now this nigga tryna act like he don't want to go to his crib and shit. He keep talking some hotel shit. What should I do?

He promptly responded:

Keep him there!

When he finished, he told Chubs to get ready. He threw the two shotguns into a large duffle bag and left the apartment. They got into a white '88 Cutlass and drove to Baum Blvd. Livewire made a right turn and parked in the Wendy's parking lot. He ran the plan down to Chubs one more time.

"When this nigga come through, I'm gonna run down on him and make him take me to the crib. You follow us. As a matter of fact, get in the driver seat now."

They switched seats. Livewire pulled the shotguns out of the bag. Five minutes later, they observed a gold-colored Lexus coupe pull into the parking lot.

"Just pull over right there. I'm gonna run in and order something." said Lisa.

"I can just go through the drive thru real quick." Lex suggested.

"Nah, I know somebody who works there, so I get my shit free. Just pull over." said Lisa.

Lex pulled over and parked next to the white Cutlass Supreme. Lisa got out of the car, glanced at the Cutlass and went inside the Wendy's. Once she was safely inside, Livewire exited the car. He had the shotty at his side pinned against his leg. He opened the passenger door of the Lexus and got in.

"Don't make me splatter ya ass, nigga. Put ya hands on the steering wheel."

Lex complied with the demand. Livewire patted him down checking for weapons. He didn't find any. Lisa had assured him that Lex didn't have a gun on him, but he would rather be safe than sorry.

"Look, nigga. I ain't gonna play no games with you, Lex."

Lex looked surprised that this strange dude knew his name.

"Yeah, I know ya name *and* I know where you live. Out in Duquesne, right?" He asked rhetorically. "That's exactly where we going right now. Drive!" said Livewire.

Lex felt a lump in his throat. The steering wheel felt slippery under his sweaty palms. He proceeded to drive home with a sickly feeling in his stomach as Chubs followed close behind. When they arrived at Lex's house in Duquesne, Livewire took the key from Lex and made him get out. They went inside the house where his girlfriend was watching TV in an upstairs bedroom as their newborn daughter slept in her crib. They quickly detained them both. Chubs checked the rest of the house to see if anyone else was present. In the bedroom, Lex was playing stupid like he didn't know the combination to the safe.

"Fuck this shit! Everybody downstairs now!" said an irritated Livewire.

The girlfriend picked up the baby. They all went downstairs, where Livewire led them into the kitchen. He went over to the stove and turned on the oven to 350 degrees. He frantically searched through the cabinets until he found what he was looking for. Livewire sat the roasting pan on top of the stove and approached the girlfriend.

"Give me the baby." said Livewire.

"I'm not giving you my baby." she said and began to cry.

"I'm not gonna hurt the baby, but I will shoot you, if you don't' do what I say." Livewire threatened.

Reluctantly, she handed over the baby while weeping. He took the sleeping baby and placed her in the roasting pan then placed the roasting pan inside the oven and closed the door.

"Nooooo!" screamed the woman as she made an attempt to rush to her baby's rescue. Her attempt was met by a violent blow to the head from the butt of Livewire's shotgun. The blow knocked her unconscious to the floor.

"Now stop fucking around! If you don't hurry up and open that safe, ya baby will fucking bake! I think you should hurry before that shit gets hot." said Livewire.

"Aight man! I'll open it!" said Lex.

"Stay here and watch her." Livewire told Chubs.

He took Lex upstairs, where he quickly opened the safe, revealing its contents. Livewire's eyes grew wide at the sight of all the cash. Had his eyes been wide with attentiveness instead of greed, he would've noticed the red and blue lights silently twirling through the front window of the room. Livewire turned his gun on Lex and shot him twice in the chest.

Boom! Boom!

Chubs was still downstairs holding the woman at gunpoint. They both heard the booms of the shotgun blast and the girlfriend climbed to her feet screaming frantically trying to make a run for it. Chubs took aim with his shotgun and squeezed the trigger, unleashing a deafening thunder throughout the kitchen.

Chubs ran out of the kitchen and hurdled the girlfriend's body that was sprawled out on the floor. His adrenaline was pumping overtime. He never noticed the red and blue lights flashing outside the house. It turned out that Lex had been having trouble with nosey neighbors. They were an older interracial couple. The wife was always looking out the window. At 68 years old, she was a retired security guard who never made the force. She would call the police, if Lex pulled up in his car with the music blasting or if too many people were going in and out of the house. Once, she called the police to break up a family barbecue in Lex's backyard.

When Lex pulled up in his driveway, true to form, his nosey neighbor was sitting in her chair, peeking through the curtains. She watched Chubs as he exited the Cutlass. She knew that her eyes weren't deceiving her and the two men she didn't recognize were carrying shotguns. Her police instinct kicked in. She immediately dialed 911 and reported what she saw.

Livewire heard the blast from Chubs shotgun as he finished emptying the safe. He slung the duffle bag over his shoulder and quickly left the room. He galloped down the stairs to where Chubs was waiting for him at the landing.

"You took care of that bitch, right?" asked Livewire.

"Yeah, I took care of it."

"Aight, let's bounce."

Livewire opened the door and stepped out onto the porch in a hurry. The sight before him almost made him shit in his pants. It looked as if half of the city's police force was in front of the house. He looked shockingly at Chubs who was standing to his right with nervousness written across his face and fear in his eyes. Livewire knew if he allowed himself to be captured, he would never see the light of day,again. Everything flashed before his eyes in a second. The fact that he was caught red-handed for a robbery, home invasion, and double murder. He coupled all of that with the fact Chubs was a minor and the baby forgotten in the oven. He would take the bulk of the weight. He would become John Allen Muhammad. He was sure to get the death penalty. A single tear escaped his left tear duct and he knew what he had to do.

"Freeze motherfucker! Put the gun down and put your hands over your head!" yelled one police officer. His face twisted into an angry scowl as he said his statement with conviction.

Livewire looked around for an escape and weighed his options one more time.

"Put the fucking guns down now!"

Livewire raised his shotgun, but was unable to get off a single shot before he was cut down in a hail of bullets. The police force fired a total of 227 shots killing both Livewire and Chubs.

***

Psycho was seated on the couch at his mother's townhome. She still resided in subsidized housing in Oak Hill. In spite of all the money, Psycho had managed to make, he still had yet to purchase a house for himself. He was the kind of person to get stuck in the hood, even with the means to make it out. He learned this behavior from his mother. Just like her son, she didn't want to leave the hood either.

Psycho was accompanied by Stickman and Taliban as usual. There were two blunts of kush being passed around amongst the three of them. Stickman had a blunt in his left hand and the TV remote control in his right hand, surfing through the channels.

"Yo, go back!" said Psycho.

"What?"

"Go back, nigga! Go back!" repeated Psycho.

"Go back to what?"

"The news!"

Stickman went back three channels, until he found what was making Psycho so excited. It was a WPXI broadcast. They missed the beginning, but were able to catch the bulk of the story:

"All the details still aren't clear as far as motives are concerned. Police are hinting at the possibility of a home invasion robbery. There was a bag found in the possession of one of the two assailants containing money and jewelry. Both have been pronounced dead after police say there was an exchange of gunfire. The police found the body of one of the victims in an upstairs bedroom.

A woman's body was also discovered in the kitchen. She appears to have suffered a gunshot wound to the back. Police say, when they found her she was mumbling the words, "my baby... my baby" and pointing at the stove. Police officers received quite a shock when they opened the oven and found a six-month-old baby girl cooking. Police quickly removed the child who looked to have suffered 3rd-degree burns to the entire backside of her head and body. We won't know for sure until we get a report from the hospital. Unfortunately, the woman succumbed to her injuries before EMS could arrive.

This is such a tragedy here in this neighborhood."

Psycho couldn't get the answers he wanted so he got on the computer. He logged onto the city's local crime website to get more authentic information. He found out the identity of both men killed by the police. He learned one of them was a minor named Harold "Chubs" Turner. They even included a photo of him at his eighth grade graduation.

"Damn! That young nigga wilded out!" said Taliban.

"Hell yeah." agreed Psycho. He continued to read and what came next was enough to make him choke on kush smoke.

"The other man has been identified as Michael "Livewire" Scott…" Livewire's photo appeared on the page. Psycho was stunned. Once he regained his composure, he began to speak.

"Yo, that's the nigga we was looking for right there." said Psycho.

"Hell yeah! That's that nigga." responded Stickman.

"I wanted to spank that nigga myself, but *dead is dead*. So, fuck it. One less nigga we gotta worry about." said Taliban.

They all erupted in laughter.

Psycho was staring at the screen in a weed induced haze as if he were in some sort of trance. He collected his thoughts before he spoke.

"Yo, that's Gunz right-hand man, right? And that nigga gonna be sick, he lost his main shooter, right? So more than likely, he'll be at the funeral to mourn this nigga." He was talking more to himself than anyone else.

"Yup." answered Taliban. He knew Psycho well enough to know exactly what he was thinking, but for sheer pleasure he asked anyhow.

"Why? What are you thinking?" asked Taliban.

Chapter 20

Detectives Collins and Novak were following up on some leads in Homestead when they heard the call come across their radio.

"Shot's fired!"

All units were told to respond.

Duquesne is a neighboring borough of Homestead. The detectives arrived there in the nick of time. With sirens blaring, they sped toward the scene in their late model Chevy Impala. When they reached the crime scene, they had to push past a throng of news reporters and onlookers. They stepped over the corpses of the two assailants sprawled out on the porch. They entered the house and were debriefed by an officer. The first thing Detective Collins noticed was the trail of blood leading from the hallway into the kitchen. It looked like a body had been dragged. After piecing together the clues received from the reporting officers, he was able to surmise that the woman was shot running from the kitchen, which was evident from the gunshot wound to the back and the shell casing found on the kitchen floor.

"After the shooter fled, the woman must have crawled back into the kitchen to save her baby from the oven." said Collins. "What kind of sick fuck puts a little baby in an oven? It's a little baby for Christ's sake!"

"Yeah," agreed Novak. "I wish we could've taken those sons of a bitches alive. At least that dickhead, Scott. I had plans to bury his ass under the jail. He's the one they call Livewire."

"Isn't that the same guy from the shooting on Centre Ave, recently?" asked Novak.

"Yup, that's him. You know how it goes. This week's suspect is next week's victim. Fuck 'em." he spat.

It turned out that Livewire used a .44 magnum during the murders on Centre, which didn't leave behind any shell casings because it's a revolver. Both guns used that night belonged to him and he took the liberty of loading the weapons. The mistake was that he neglected to use any gloves while loading the weapons and his fingerprints turned up on the shell casings, ejected from the Glock .40 found at the scene. They were consistent with the caliber of the bullets the victims were killed with. There had been a warrant issued for his arrest, but police had yet to discover his whereabouts, until he exited the front door of Lex's house wielding a shotgun.

During the investigation, it was learned that Scott had a friend with whom he was almost inseparable, Calvin "Junior" Summers. They knew it was a 90% chance Junior was with him when he committed the murders on Centre Ave. But before they could apprehend him and bring him in for questioning, he was gunned down. The detectives thought Junior's killing was retaliation for the Centre Ave killings, but with only circumstantial evidence and no further leads to follow, the case fizzled out. Collins and Novak, however, would continue to investigate.

The days leading up to Livewire's funeral were heavy on Gunz. The realization of losing his best shooter was devastating for him. Sure, he was very much *willing* to put in the necessary work for his crew. But was he *capable?* He had to admit to himself, albeit never to anyone else. The truth was that he wasn't as good as he used to be. He was older, slower and beginning to develop cold feet. He knew he couldn't get things in order by himself. He would need some help, some young, energetic, borderline crazy help. The problem was he couldn't think of a single person who would fit the bill. Losing both, Junior *and* Livewire, was a bigger blow than he had ever imagined. It became clear to him at the wake. Gunz attended to view the body and pay respect. Immediately afterward, he began scouting the crowd for any young faces, he may've recognized. He was hopeful to find some impressionable young boys excited about the possibility of taking Livewire's place. He had conversations with a couple guys and decided to try some of them out, until he could find better. He just hoped they would last long enough. But more than that, he hoped he would last long enough himself.

The kind of pressure Psycho and Body had been able to apply made Gunz nervous. He could see nervousness etched in his own face as he looked in the mirror to adjust his tie. Livewire's funeral was beginning in an hour. It was being held in Homewood at Shiloh Community Missionary Baptist Church on Frankstown Road. Gunz felt like he needed to show camaraderie and solidarity to his crew. A move to show that he would be there for them until the end. He decided to foot the bill for the entire funeral and huge headstone for Livewire. He also arranged for his family to ride in a stretch Lincoln

Towncar limousine, prepared an assortment of flowers and volunteered to be a pallbearer. He even hired a DJ for the repass to send his man off *in style*. He knew that was the sadistic display of love the youth wanted to see and obliged. His last order of business was convincing Marv' to show up to the funeral and be a pallbearer as well.

"Man, we need to show these young niggas that we care, if we ever expect their loyalty and expect them to execute orders efficiently. If they get the sense that we don't give a fuck, it's only natural that they won't give a fuck either." said Gunz.

Surprisingly enough for him, he didn't have to say much to convince Marv'. He knew that Gunz was absolutely correct in his statement. He didn't put up any resistance. He agreed. He figured it was a good idea and had to be done. When the day finally arrived, he just wanted to get it over with as quickly as possible.

Marv' and Gunz rode to the church in a Lincoln Towncar limousine of their own. When they arrived, the church parking lot was filled to capacity. There weren't any parking spaces on the street either. Livewire's funeral drew a larger than expected crowd. The limo driver had to double park on the street and wait for them to depart to the church.

The funeral proceedings weren't anything out of the ordinary. The preacher gave a lengthy sermon about the importance of celebrating the memory of life, instead of grieving death. One of Livewire's relatives read off his eulogy. His mama and baby mama cried rivers and dramatically draped themselves over his casket, until they were physically removed. The preacher announced the last viewing of the body and the casket was closed. The casket was a mahogany color with brass handles and an eggshell white, silk lining.

Marv' and Gunz took their positions among the other pallbearers and led the funeral procession outside. They emerged from the church first and headed toward the awaiting hearse. No one noticed the Jeep Cherokee double parked a few cars lengths away. As they descended the church stairs, the Cherokee slowly crept forward in stealth mode. Just as the pallbearers were preparing to load the casket into the hearse, their attention was drawn to a melee breaking out in the back of the crowd. Everyone turned with appalled looks as the scene unfolded. One man yelled with conviction at another, "*Nigga, get ya hand out my pocket!*"

Tempers began to flare quickly at their audacity to act like that at Livewire's funeral. While their focus was on that, both passenger doors of the Cherokee opened up and two men hopped out brandishing a pair of Mac 90's. They were intimidating machines with a striking resemblance to an AK 47. It even fired the same 7.62 rounds. Before, anyone had an opportunity to react, the two masked gunmen opened fire on the group of pallbearers. As if on cue, the man who created the distraction pulled a shotgun from beneath his trench coat and began firing on the pallbearers, as well. His main job was to make sure Marv' and Gunz didn't get away.

As if a gift from the War Gods, the first two pallbearers were Marv' and Gunz. The two assassins opened fire with the high powered rifles causing the pallbearers to drop the casket. The impact of the fall caused the coffin to splinter and the lock to jolt open. Livewire's body tumbled out of the casket and rolled a few feet away. Gunz and Marv' laid slain at the curbside. The excessive amount of shots they received made them unrecognizable. The overkill was a statement. All of the men jumped into the Cherokee and fled the scene.

Chapter 21

Body was laying in the bed with Mila rubbing her belly. It seemed to be growing daily. She was nearly five months and looked like she could pop any day. He was applying *A Mother's Nature* cream to her stomach to prevent stretch marks. She was channel surfing.

"What's the sense of having cable, if there's never shit on? Maybe, we should get some kind of satellite package or something. It probably won't make much difference, other than sports." said Mila.

"That's cool cause I like sports."

"Yeah, me too and I can watch *my* futbol games."

"Here you go with that soccer shit. That ain't no real football. Does Puerto Rico even have a team?" asked Body while laughing.

"Yeah, we have a team nigga. Don't be tryna play us like that." she said with a sexy Latina accent rolling her eyes.

"Let me see what's on the news first."

Mila obliged and turned to the news. KDKA was broadcasting the day's hot story. Body sat up in the bed and listened more intently. He was shocked at the information. He was learning about that morning's event. They coined it "The Frankstown Massacre". Body learned that five people were killed and six others were injured. Police were offering a $50,000 reward for anyone with information leading to an arrest and conviction. The Mayor held a press conference expressing his outrage and offering his condolences to families of the victims.

"Stupid motherfuckers!" yelled Body.

"Baby, what's wrong?" asked Mila puzzled.

Body ignored her. He got out of the bed and began dressing. He was off in his own thoughts and his anger didn't allow him to hear whatever it was that Mila was saying to him. He continued to get dressed and mumbled to himself.

"Dumb ass niggas gonna get us all knocked. How stupid can you be? Told these niggas! We don't need no heat right now."

Body finished lacing up his *Timberlands*, grabbed his keys and cell phone off the nightstand. He was out the door.

***

Stickman walked into the Oakland condominium where Psycho, Taliban and Man Man were waiting.

"Yo, it's hot as hell out there. Fucking twelve everywhere!"

"Did you get rid of the car?" asked Psycho.

"Hell yeah, I got rid of that shit. I was already prepared before shit went down. I did what you told me. I had another whip parked near the spot where I dumped the dirty ride. It had a canister of gasoline in it already. I torched that bitch like I always do." said Stickman.

"Aight, cool. Shit is gonna be a little hot for a while, so we gotta be extra careful. They want somebody's head on the guillotine for this shit. So, make sure ya'll don't say *shit* to anybody outside this room, about what happened." said Psycho.

"You already know." responded Taliban.

"Yo, that idea you came up with was genius, Psych. I wasn't sure if that shit was gonna work, but it was perfect. What made you think of some shit like that?" asked Man Man.

"Shit, it was Body's idea." Psycho chuckled.

"I thought Body didn't know what was going on?" asked Stickman in confusion.

"Nah, he didn't know nothing. But, you know how he likes kicking that black history. One day he was telling me the story about Malcolm X and how he got spanked. While he was giving his speech, somebody yelled, *Nigger, get ya hands out my pockets!* Everybody diverted their attention to what was going on, even the security. Then, niggas drew down on Malcolm. I never forgot that story. It just came to my mind when I was trying to figure out the best way to creep up on them niggas. I wanted to be as close as possible, before they realized it. Them niggas wasn't gonna be giving no speeches. So, the funeral was the best thing I could come up with." said Psycho.

In mid-conversation, Body strolled into the condo. It was easy to determine the mood he was in by the scowl he was wearing on his face.

"What's good, Ike?" said Psycho.

"That fucking $50,000 bounty they got out on niggas. That's what's good. How could ya'll niggas be so dumb? That was some stupid ass shit! Everything we have going for ourselves right now and ya'll wanna fuck it up, before we even get it off the ground. I know we had to get them niggas, but not like that." said Body.

"Relax, Bro. We were extra careful and nobody outside of this room knows shit. Everything will continue to go as scheduled. We don't have to worry about shutting down shop cause that shit happened in Homewood and we ain't got no business over there. So, fuck it. Them niggas over there just gotta deal with that heat 'til it die down. Better them than us." said Psycho.

"How can you be so sure that nobody knows shit? Cause $50,000 is a lot of motivation to get niggas talking." said Body.

"Come on, bro. *You* ain't even know what was slapping. You think we told somebody else? I did exactly what you asked me to do. I ended a war that could've had a tremendous impact on our business *and our lives*. That shit was hurting our reputation and reputation is everything. *Guard it with your life*." he said *quoting the 48 Laws Of Power*.

"You taught me that." said Psycho.

"You still have to be smart, my nigga. That move could bring federal heat. The kind of heat that will have a big impact on the bottom line, the *dollar*. We still have a commitment to satisfy the plug. This could fuck everything up. Our reputation is already intact, my nigga. But our empire could crumble." said Body.

Psycho now understood the ramifications behind his brazen act. He was in the mode of a warlord out for a victory in battle. All he knew was to "*enter into action with boldness*." After hearing his right hand man's perspective, he knew that battle could cost them the war.

"I'll get up with ya'll niggas later." said Body before exiting.

Body was feeling some sort of way, but his anger was preventing him from expressing it correctly. So, he just bounced. He was experiencing a conundrum and he would have to find his balance. How does he convey his message to his boys without chastising or scolding them like children? How does he let them know that he is pissed, but he still had their backs? These were the questions he pondered. For now, he would take a long drive to clear his mind and figure out his next step. But, he was sure that the latest killings would eventually bring more trouble than they were prepared to deal with. He knew what he had to do. He had to get out the game, while he was still ahead. He had enough money to fall back. The game wasn't going anywhere, *if or when* he was ready to jump back in. He didn't need to take unnecessary risks like hustling in the midst of such heat. He would just go underground on niggas, he thought. Maybe, he would go back to school. Maybe, he could even pick back up where he left off with basketball. He had a high school diploma and an 1100 SAT score. It shouldn't be too difficult for him to gain admittance to college. He knew he wanted to be in business, but what kind of business. He was unsure. Mila was a business major. She would be able to assist him, which gave him more confidence. She was the first person to teach him how to incorporate. She wanted to see him win. She would make sure of it. His mind was considering a million things at once and he began to develop a migraine. His temples were pounding and he couldn't escape his own thoughts.

What he wanted was something legitimate that would earn him enough money to leave the drug game once and for all. His savings would help make that possible, when the time came. For the moment, he would concentrate on his business and figure out how to move shipments out of Miami. He never had an opportunity to share his ideas with Psycho after their trip. Even though he didn't want to be bothered with him right now, there was business at hand that needed to be attended to. The first shipment was moving pretty quickly and they didn't have any time to waste. He pulled out his cell phone and gave Psycho a call.

"Yo." Psycho answered.

"Yo, what's good? We need to talk real quick." said Body.

"I hope it ain't 'bout the same shit." replied Psycho.

"Man, later for that shit. I got something important to run past you. Where you at?" asked Body.

"The same place you left me." replied Psycho.

"Aight, I'll be there in a few minutes."

Body made a detour and headed toward the Oakland condo, where he had just confronted his crew a few hours earlier. When he arrived, everybody was in the living room playing Playstation 3. Psycho looked up from his game and made eye contact with Body. Body gave him a sideways nod indicating that he wanted Psycho to come to him. Body then began walking up the stairs and Psycho paused the game.

"Yo, don't touch my game. I'm coming right back. Imma finish kicking ya ass."

"Yeah, whatever nigga just hurry up 'cause it's fourth down now." replied Taliban.

Psycho headed up the stairs and entered the room where Body was waiting.

"What's good?" he asked, as they gave each other dap and embraced in a manly hug.

"We need to get shit situated with this work. We gotta drop off the money we owe and pick up the next shipment. But, we never discussed how we're gonna move work out of hot ass Florida." said Body.

"I was just thinking 'bout the same shit, Bro. But I don't know how to do that shit." said Psycho.

"Well I have an idea. We can hire a transport company. They transport cars all over the country. Or we can just buy our own, something with a twelve car capacity. That way, we have full control of the shipments. We can provide the cheapest bids and ensure that we have cars to move whenever we need to get a shipment out of Miami. Since all the paperwork is legit for the transport, the driver can play dumb about the contents of the car he's carrying. Once we get it out of Florida it'll land in Charlotte, North Carolina. From there, we'll pack that shit in stash box vans and have it delivered back here." said Body. His wheels had begun to turn.

"Yo, that shit sounds official." said Psycho.

"Aight, bet. I'm gonna put everything in motion and I'll tell you how much I need from you later, so we can get this company going and pay the driver. I'll probably buy open transport vehicles because they're cheaper than the enclosed ones." said Body.

"Aight, just let me know." said Psycho.

With that, Body departed from the condo. He wanted to get a jump start on his tasks. It was of extreme importance to execute everything with perfection and have all the small details down to a science. He would take on the challenge of making sure that's exactly what was gonna happen. His future depended on it.

Chapter 22

Detectives Collins and Novak had been hard at work with their investigation. They had learned quite a bit of information from snitches. They knew about the feud between Body, Marv' and Gunz. Although, they weren't aware of how it originated. They suspected that there was a connection between Junior's murder and the double homicide on Centre Avenue. They pondered over the probability that this was all related. Collins and Novak had developed, what they called, a *nose* for big cases. Something smells fishy and they would sniff it out.

"Seems that all this shit is stemming from some sort of war. We know who Marv was. Everybody knew Marv and Gunz. So, who had enough muscle and balls to take them to war...and *win*? What are we dealing with here, partner? Cartel, maybe?" Novak's mind was churning.

"Not sure. What I do know, is that fat piece of shit, Marv', was a no good, dope dealing, scumbag. We've been trying to get something on him for the past decade. I'm glad somebody finally was able to do what we couldn't. I pulled some tricks out of my bag and that fat bastard still managed to slip away. He was one *smart* son of a bitch. I'll give him that." said Collins.

Anyone who was conscious was aware that Detectives Collins and Novak were two detectives to be feared. It was common knowledge. They were willing to fabricate and plant evidence to receive their desired outcome. Most people found it wise to stay out of their way and avoid them at all cost, if possible. If they believed that you were guilty of a crime, then they would judge you accordingly and tamper with the evidence to ensure conviction. They didn't leave it up to chance. The problem was, nobody is always right. *Many* years of incarceration had been served unjustly. If their skeletons were ever revealed, it may topple the Western Pennsylvania Judicial System. They couldn't tolerate something like that now... Could they?

"We're gonna crack this case open. I can feel it. The only problem is, we have no positive ID, not even a good partial. We have to apply a little pressure and shake shit up a bit. They'll fold like the bitches they truly are and we'll know exactly who was involved. What do we know about them?" asked Novak.

"We know they're led by Jabar Jones, the one called *Body*. So, the first order of business should be getting something to stick on Jones. If we kill the head, the *body* dies, too." They chuckled at the double entendre.

"If he's anything like most of these new era gangsters, he'll be talking until we have to slap him to keep quiet." said Collins.

Chapter 23

Body successfully put his plan into motion and everything went accordingly. The car transport company won the bid to do business in Miami, Florida. The pickup and drop off went smoothly. Jesus sent word that he was impressed with the amount of time they were able to move, such a large shipment. It took three weeks for them to get rid of the entire package. In that amount of time, they were able secure four additional locations to trap from. They had a place on the North Side, East Hills, West End and Mckeesport. Each spot was able to move close to a whole bird per day. That equaled four birds per day on the ground.

They were seeing some serious money, but it didn't prevent them from setting their sights higher. They had deals worked out with niggas from all over the city to set up shop in their neighborhoods. To provide all the work and split profits with them. Body came up with the idea. He viewed it as a franchising opportunity. He figured, if he could create ways for others to eat, it would bring him untold wealth. Psycho, however, didn't like the idea of having to split 50/50 with some niggas that he could easily overpower. But for now, he would go along with the plan.

Body thought about the rapid pace, which the business was growing and he knew they would need heavier loads soon. He realized that his leverage would change because of his capacity to move large quantities, quickly. He was listening while Jesus was talking in Colombia and he learned fast. He would renegotiate his deal with Jesus. He figured he could get another thousand dollars knocked off each bird for the kind of success he was obtaining. If that didn't sound like much, it put an additional $150,000 in his pocket. Maybe, he would use it to purchase flight time aboard a private jet and have that shit flown back. He loved to have options. Now, he had to inform Psycho of his decisions, so they would be on the same page.

"I already told you about the new number we got from Jesus, but we need more than one way to move this work. So, check out what I did. I got us a private jet. We'll be flying under the name of a corporation. That way our frequent flights look like business trips. They ask you to give two hours notice, but they say they're able to provide us with a jet nationwide. We can get a nice size jet for $150,000 and fifty hours of travel time.

"Ahh shit! We 'bout to be riding G5's and shit." said Psycho.

"One day we will, my nigga." responded Body. "We're going with something smaller. It was a good rate and it's convenient to do fractional ownership. We save money that way. We can upgrade the package, whenever we want. But, fifty hours will get us eight trips. That means we pay $18,750 per load. That's $125 a bird." Body laughed. "Why haven't we *been* thought of this shit?" he asked rhetorically.

"Yeah, it makes all the sense in the world." Psycho agreed. "It's a cheaper rate than we're paying now. I told you that you're a genius, Bro. I guess we can re-up on the time cards too, right?" asked Psycho.

"Yeah, we can buy time in fifty hour blocks, a hundred, a hundred and fifty, so on and so forth. The charter company is called *Jet*

Smart. I'm gonna fly to Atlanta this weekend for a test run. We need to fill the situation out, so we know exactly what's going on. I copped a few *Hugo Boss* suits today and a briefcase, too. I have to look like I work for the corporation that our flight time is registered under. It's called *International Financial Management Corporation*. That shit sounds official, right?" They giggled together like school kids.

"Hell yeah. That shit sounds like big business." said Psycho.

"It is big business, nigga. I'm 'bout to go prepare for my trip and I'll let you know what it's hitting for as soon as I get back." said Body.

With that, the two men parted ways. Body went straight home and began packing his bags. He was excited about getting away for the weekend. He had never been to Atlanta before, but he always wanted to visit and he planned to make the best of this trip. Of course, he would focus on the task at hand. But, it wouldn't take much to complete and he needed a vacation, too. There were a lot of things going on in his life with the pregnancy and the larger shipments. Plus, *"The Frankstown Massacre"* had him on pins and needles. He just wanted to unwind for a couple days and try his best not to think of any of those things.

Once all of his bags were packed and he was ready to go, he called a jitney to pick him up. The jitney would take him to the small airport on the outskirts of the city that catered to non-commercial flights. Body called a jitney driver, who he knew personally, Fast Bob. He used to take Body all over the city, before he had his own car. Fast Bob never had him wait more than ten minutes for pick up.

It would've normally taken forty minutes to drive to the airport, but Fast Bob did it in twenty five. When he arrived, he scoped out his surroundings. The jet was fully fueled and waiting on the tarmac. It was a Piaggio Avanti. He gave his name, recited his account number, showed the required documents and boarded the plane. He met the pilot and co-pilot. Then, he relaxed in his seat and enjoyed a vodka and cranberry. He hadn't had much sleep for a few nights and the comfortable leather seat got the best of him as he dozed off.

When he was awakened by the stewardess, it was a few hours later. He was already in Atlanta. When he got off the plane there was a chauffeured Cadillac Escalade from a local company waiting for him. The chauffeur took Body's suitcase and loaded it into the trunk. Body let himself into the back seat of the car while the driver secured his luggage. He considered it *bourgeois* to wait for the chauffeur to come open his door after he loaded the trunk. This wasn't a limo ride to a special event after all, he thought. He would have to get acclimated to the finer things in life. He was taken downtown to the Hilton Atlanta. He tipped the driver and allowed the bellhop to take his luggage. He went to the front desk to retrieve the key card for the room he reserved under the company's name. Once he got to his room, he tipped the bellhop. He was a young black guy who Body figured could give him pertinent information about the area.

"What's some of the best spots to hit down here on the club scene?" asked Body.

"Well, you might wanna check out *Magic City*. It's not too far from here. And it's right across the street from the bus station, so you'll be able to find it easily." he said with a southern accent. "You can also check out, *Strokers*. That's a good one."

"Aight, good-looking." he said, giving the bellhop a pound and extra $20.

"Aight, shawty." he responded, before turning and leaving out the door.

***

While Body was in Atlanta having a good time, Psycho was back home getting things situated with all the new territory they managed to branch out to. He was also in the process of closing on a business deal that he had been working on. The moves that Body had been making were beginning to inspire Psycho. But, behind every seemingly good idea was an evil ulterior motive.

Psycho purchased a building in the neighboring county of Butler. The building was an old crematory and still had all of its original equipment. Psycho planned to use the building for exactly what it was designed, *cremation*. He would put the business in the name of one of his relatives, who would run all of the daily operations of the business. He would make a few legitimate dollars, but the business would serve a dual purpose for Psycho.

Growing up in the hood, like many black youth, Psycho was infatuated with gangster personas from gangster movies. He watched how mobsters from Italy, Russia, China and abroad would get rid of the bodies when they killed someone.

"That's how I would do it, if I had to spank somebody." he would say while watching movies like *Casino*.

Now the time had come when he was committing murder himself. He would have his own creative way of disposing bodies. Psycho would live up to his name and cremate his victims and discard the remains. He already did the necessary research. He knew that a body needed to burn over 1,400 degrees for two and a half hours in order to have a proper cremation. Otherwise, there would be residue and that would lead to DNA. After the fire burns off all the water a body contains and burns through the organs and tissue, you're left with the skeleton. The bones needed time to cool before putting them into the processing machine to be grinded up. The bones would be processed until the consistency of ash. Those were some of the things that Psycho had learned from the old man, who sold him the building. He knew Body was right about the way he handled the war with Marv' and Gunz. It made a lot of noise, *too* much noise. If he survived the blunder, he would be much smarter going forward. He was ready to elevate his game. He was also ready to sever ties with some business associates. To him, severing those ties equalled death. He wanted to take over territories like Hannibal and some of the other great conquerors that Body taught him about. The idea itself was evil, but brilliant.

Chapter 24

The tires came to a screeching halt as the jet landed. Body had returned from Atlanta. His flight was comfortable and there was no turbulence. He sat attentively, staring out of the window observing the surroundings. Flying private sure had its perks. It was like living in the suburbs as opposed to the projects. The further out you go away from the inner city the less police presence you see. Just as when he first boarded the plane, police presence was virtually non-existent. Afterall, this was a private airport. The only thing they had to be worried about was being FAA compliant with their take off and landing, which any competent pilot could do. Body sat in the lobby eating snacks from the vending machines while waiting for Fast Bob. He called Psycho to schedule an immediate meeting to discuss his flight experience. He pulled out his cell phone and dialed the number.

Ring! Ring! Ring!

"Yo?" answered Psycho.

"What's the drill, Bro? I just got back and I'm close to town. Where you at?" asked Body.

"I'm at the condo. Swing through." said Psycho.

"Aight. I'll be there in a few ticks." said Body.

Body hit the end button and terminated the call. Twenty minutes later, he was at the condo. He paid the jitney handsomely with $200 for the trip and an additional $100 to wait for him. He went inside where the whole gang were sitting around the table gambling in a game of Tonk. All the men greeted Body with brotherly love and he reciprocated.

"What's good, Bro? How was ATL?" asked Taliban.

"That shit was official. We all gotta go down there sometime. I didn't wanna come back." said Body.

"Damn, it was popping like that?" asked Man Man.

"Hell yea! It was popping everywhere I went, *Magic City, Strokers, Body Tap*. There's some bad ass women down there and niggas was stunting hard, too. They had all kinds of whips down that bitch, Bentleys, Ferraris, Lambos, Maseratis. That shit was motivation, my nigga."

"Them niggas playing real hard down there, huh?" asked Psycho.

"I'm telling you, Ike. Next time I go, I'm having everything set up. So, we can push some foreign shit down there. They rent everything down there. Fuck around get a Bugatti!"

"Yo, I'm getting the Phantom!" exclaimed Man Man.

"Man, I wish we could cop shit like that around here. You come through this bitch in a Lambo, you're going straight to jail." said Psycho.

"Do not pass go! Do not collect $200!" added Taliban.

"I just might be crazy enough to do that shit though." said Psycho.

"Yeah, you just might be crazy enough to get us all indicted, nigga." said Body seriously.

He needed his man to know that a move like that wasn't okay. They went back and forth for the next forty minutes, before Body filled everyone in on his flight and they listened with intrigue. He described to them in great detail, everything about his private flight experience from the moment he entered the premises to the time he exited. He told them about the plan he devised for transporting on the jets. Everyone understood what was taking place. Body was satisfied with his progress. He was ready to climb into his own bed. He had been at the condo for over two hours and lost track of time. He realized that Fast Bob was still outside waiting for him. He dapped up everyone before leaving. His ride was waiting, patiently. For the amount of money, he made per hour when he was with Body, he didn't have any room for complaints.

"Sorry to keep you waiting so long." said Body as he passed him two crispy one-hundred dollar bills.

"Don't worry about it, young buck." Fast Bob said with a swift response. Waiting for Body paid a lot better than his other job over at the *Spaghetti Factory*.

Body was anxious to get home to Mila. Even though she got on his nerves at times, he loved her dearly. Plus, he knew that her emotions were due to the pregnancy. While he was in Atlanta, she called him continuously. Not that she wanted anything in particular. She just wanted to feel like she had his attention. Of course, he played along. He didn't want the kind of problems *not playing along* would bring him when he returned home.

The entire ride his loins were fueled with the excitement of getting close to Mila. He wanted to smell her, to kiss her, to taste her. Her pregnancy made her more desirable to him. It was true. The love of a woman was *better* when she's pregnant.

He reflected on his life and had to admit he felt pretty good, overall. He had a beautiful, smart, loyal woman. He was about to be a new father. He was quickly elevating in the game and had a nice nest egg to support his family. Just the thought of all the positive things in his life brought a smile to his face.

As he turned onto his street, the smile he wore was immediately replaced with a look of concern. He looked in disbelief at the red and blue flashing lights and cluster of police cars in front of his home. The first emotion to register was worry. He worried that something may have happened to Mila. He quickly dismissed that from his mind as he assessed the scene and didn't see any ambulance or coroner presence. That ruled out the possibility of anyone being hurt or dead. He was still a little worried. Naturally because he was unaware of why the police were there. He didn't see any federal agents. What could it be? He thought.

"You want me to keep driving, young buck? You know I ain't gonna turn you over to the fuzz." said Bob.

"Nah, man. I gotta make sure wifey's straight. Plus, aint shit in there, anyway. Never been one to shit where I lay my head." said Body.

"Smart man. Be safe, young buck. I'm gone." said Fast Bob as he pulled up to the house next to an unmarked police car.

"Aight take it easy, Bob."

As Fast Bob pulled off, Body began walking towards his house, mentally preparing himself for the inevitable upcoming confrontation. Before he could reach the front door, he was stopped by two uniformed cops.

"Hold it right there, sir. Do you live here?" asked the officer to his immediate right.

He was a young Italian named, Leoni, who didn't look a day over twenty five.

"Yeah, I live here with my wife. Is there a problem?" asked Body.

"We'll ask all the fucking questions." came the snide reply from the officer to his left. They were playing *good cop bad cop* already, Body thought. The cop looked to be in his forties. Some prick with too many syllables in his name for Body to even try pronouncing. He guessed that the name was Polish.

"What's your name?" asked the Polish prick.

"Jabar Jones."

"Well now, you're just the little shit we've been waiting for. You're under arrest." said the cop.

"For what?"

Before he had a chance to respond, Body saw Homicide Detectives Collins and Novak emerging from inside the house. Detective Novak carried a rolled up paper in his right hand, which Body assumed to be a warrant.

"Well, well, well if it ain't Mr. Body." said a smiling Novak as he approached confidently.

Body stared into the weather-beaten face of the detective. His skin appeared to be leather from too many trips to the tanning booth.

"Let me do the honors and read this fucker his rights." said Novak.

He grabbed Body by the shoulder and spun him around while violently twisting his arm behind his back and cuffing him. Body didn't resist.

"You're under arrest for the murder of Darius Packard." said the detective, like he was handing out an award instead of making an arrest.

"You have the right to remain silent."

Body's mind went blank for a moment. This had to be some sort of mistake.

"You have the right to an attorney."
He had no idea who the hell Darius Packard was.

"If you cannot afford an attorney one will be provided…."
Was it somebody from *The Frankstown Massacre?*

"Do you understand these rights as they have been read to you?"

Body was only half hearing whatever it was Novak was saying. His thoughts were consumed by going to jail for murder. This was always a fear of his. He always knew there could be a possibility, but he was bewildered because he didn't know what the police were talking about. It was one thing to have to answer for crimes that you've committed. But, what answer do you give for a crime you have no knowledge of. His mind couldn't focus in on anything at that moment.

Just before he was placed in the back of the squad car, Mila came wobbling out of the house, crying hysterically and screaming his name.

"Jabar, what's happening?" she asked frantically.

"Everything is fine baby. Just some sort of misunderstanding. Call the lawyer and tell him what's happening. I'll be out shortly, Mami. Don't worry."

He managed to say all of that as he was loaded into the car and the door abruptly slammed in his face. He turned awkwardly in his seat despite his restraints, so he could see Mila through the rear window. He watched her as the police car descended down the block. She stood curbside crying with her hands cradling her belly. Body knew she was strong. He was confident that she would be okay. They held each other's gaze until the car was no longer in view.

Once he arrived at the Allegheny County Jail, the squad car had to be buzzed in through huge metal gates resembling garage doors. They drove through the underpass and the gates immediately shut behind them. Novak and Collins got out of the car leaving Body seated in the rear. They went to the lock box on the wall and secured their firearms inside.

Body had heard of the two detectives before, but it was the first time he encountered them personally. He knew them as "Greasy and Grimy." He started to wonder which one was Greasy. He quickly realized that they were *one* and the *same*.

Collins opened the back door and gave a one word directive.

"Out!"

Body looked at the Black man with disgust as one name came to mind, *slave catcher*. He was escorted into the building where a stiff odor assaulted his nose as soon as he walked through the door. He was in a small room, about the size of a cell, he assumed. It had a metal bench and a metal detector against the wall. He would be taken through the standard procedures, before moving any further. He was ordered to take off his shoes, turn his socks inside out emptying his pockets, open his mouth and finally walk through the metal detector.

Once cleared, he was taken to a holding cell where he would wait for further processing and procedures. The foul stench in the holding cell was stronger than what he experienced earlier. There were bums and winos scattered about and the toilet in the corner didn't flush. The bums were sprawled out on the benches and floors, so Body found himself a place to stand in the corner and waited for his name to be called. Though he had never been to jail before, he knew enough to know that he would receive an arraignment the same night. As soon as the judge gave him a bond on this bullshit charge, he would be home sleeping in his own bed he thought.

After hours of waiting and endless pacing back and forth, his name was called.

"Jones!" yelled a heavy set Black female guard.
She didn't have to call him twice. He was ready to get out of that *hell hole* and home to his family.

"Darius Jones!" said the guard. There was another Jones in the bullpen and disappointment was written all over Body's face. He was left standing in the middle of the bullpen dumbfounded. He was so sure it was his time to go until the guard burst his bubble. An old wino slowly lifted himself from the floor and staggered his way to the door. Body was frustrated.

An hour and forty minutes later, the same heavyset woman reemerged.

"Jones!"

Body didn't budge this time, remembering the embarrassment he experienced a short while ago.

"Jabar Jones!" she finally said.

This time Body moved with enthusiasm. He hurdled a bum on his way to the door and went into the adjacent room to be photographed, fingerprinted and asked a series of identifying questions like, his address, place of employment, date of birth, level of education, emergency contact, etc. When finished with that, he was led to another holding cell where he would wait to be seen by a judge. Unfortunately for Body, there was more waiting to be done.

Seven hours later, he was cuffed and shackled then led to his arraignment hearing before the Honorable Judge Randle Cartright. He was an old, White man with a head full of silver hair. He had a face so plump, Body thought his ultimate demise would likely be his cholesterol. His lawyer, John Aderman, wasn't present. He was a Jewish attorney with Pittsburgh roots. He grew up in Mount Lebanon. He had an eclectic dress code and wore the brightest ties he could find. He was at the top of his class at his alma mater, Harvard Law School. He was an excellent defense attorney. He did a tenure as a federal prosecutor which made him well aware of the way they operated. He would chew this case up for sure, Body thought. *If he ever showed up.*

The judge read from the charge sheet. It was first degree homicide. In Pennsylvania, the time handed down for a homicide was just as severe as a murder charge in other states. In the commonwealth, one can serve *life without the possibility* of parole.

"How does the defendant plead?"

The judge was peering at Body over legal documents.

"Not guilty, Your Honor." swiftly replied Body in his own defense.

He looked to his right where Detectives Novak and Collins were present with the assistant from the DA's office. He wondered what they were doing there and if it was standard procedure. He kept looking toward the door hoping Aderman would rush through and save the day. Mila was seated in the courtroom behind the gate that separated defendants from spectators. Body gave her a wink. She smiled.

As if she could read his mind, she said, "I couldn't get in contact with Aderman. It was late, baby. I'll call him in a couple hours. You should be out before then. I love you."

"Uh-hem!" The Judge cleared his throat, taking back control of his courtroom. When he was certain that he had everyone's attention, he continued.

"Prosecutor, you look like you have something to add." said Judge Cartright.

The prosecutor was a thin, balding, Turkish man around 5'10". His frame looked very wiry in his oversized *Mens Warehouse* suit. He looked just like a public defender. Except, he was the state's public defender. Handling late night arraignments had to be entry level work, he thought.

"Yes, Your Honor, if I may. Due to the severity of the charges and the nature of the crime. I'm requesting that no bail is granted. I have here with me, decorated detectives that can attest to the danger this defendant poses. He is a drug trafficker, your Honor. And he is a flight risk. Nothing further."

The gavel came down and the ruling was decisive.

"Bail denied!"

Just like that, Body was on his way upstairs in a state of confusion and a state issued uniform. Tears escaped Mila's eyes, unsure of what the future may hold for her unborn child. She knew the baby would be well off financially. More important, however, was having his or her father present.

Chapter 25

The next day, Psycho received the news of Body's arrest. Mila called him frantic that he was held without bail. And she still hadn't spoken to the lawyer. Psycho did his best to get her to calm down. Being so far along in her pregnancy, he knew that she shouldn't be stressed. He also knew Body's lawyer was a canon and would eat the case. They both had prepaid lawyers on retainer in case these sort of things happened. Still, Psycho was confused because he didn't know who Darius Packard was either. *Maybe it was somebody from The Frankstown Massacre,* he thought. He quickly pushed those thoughts aside. Body hadn't participated in that, but that didn't mean *anything* in the hood, *anyway*. What else could it be? He pondered. He didn't want to jump to conclusions, so he would wait until he knew something more solid. He was sure that Mila would keep him posted each step of the way.

Body was scheduled for a Coroner's Inquest hearing the following morning. It was a judicial inquiry held by the coroner instead of a judge and would later be abolished in the state of Pennsylvania. Psycho planned to attend. He wanted firsthand knowledge of what was going on with his man. One thing for sure, something didn't seem right. For the moment, he would concentrate on business. Body's distribution ideas were brilliant and the product was moving faster than imagined. They began to branch out, recruiting new workers and making their presence felt in the most lucrative areas of the city.

Psycho had a meeting with a guy named Shark from the North Side of town. Shark was an up and coming young hustler from Northview Heights Projects, the biggest project complex on the entire North Side. Shark had a stronghold on the projects and was infamous for his short temper and violent ways. Northview Heights was a major crack selling area on the North Side. Some other areas of the North Side were known for heroin; and Northview had their hands in that, too. Psycho drove into Northview and scoped the layout. There was a security station resembling a toll booth at the entrance of the projects. It had windows on all sides making it easier for security to watch traffic in all directions. If he could get to the guard working the booth, he would be alerted to any police presence. There was no way to enter the projects without going past the station, after all.

Psycho saw huge potential in these projects. He cruised slowly in his Range Rover and watched a few fiends walking with exaggerated speed. The brisk November air didn't seem to disturb them. They wore no coats. Psycho spotted Shark's black 5 series BMW and pulled over behind it. Shark hopped out of the car and approached the passenger side of Psycho's SUV. Psycho hit the automatic lock and Shark hopped in.

"What's up, Cuz?" said Shark as he reached across to give Psycho dap.

"Aint shit."

"You ready for me, Cuz?" asked Shark, cutting straight to the chase. He wasn't really one for much small talk.

"Yeah, I got something for you. But, I didn't bring it with me. I just came to peep the scene real quick. I'll have somebody swing through with that shit in a minute." Psycho assured.

"Aight. Ya'll still gonna front me those shits, right?" asked Shark.

"Yeah. We got you."

"And Body said the number on them was 34."

"That's still the number. Don't worry, Ike. Give my people's like thirty or forty minutes and I'll have three for you. The shit is official, too. So, you shouldn't have a problem moving it. But, I'm gonna put you up on game and show you how we package our shit in vials. If you follow the blueprint, you'll be moving more than twice what you do right now." said Psycho reassuringly.

"That's what's up, Cuz! Just have ya people hit me when they get close." said Shark.

"Aight, bet."

With that, Shark got out of the car and Psycho pulled off. The wheels in his head were steady churning. Body had made a deal with Shark to sell him kilos at $34,000 a piece. After seeing the layout of the area and the amount of potential it possessed, Psycho began devising his own plan immediately. He would put Shark up on game, so that the block's proceeds would substantially increase. Then, he would take it all for himself. He felt like Shark didn't know what to do with the Heights. He also knew that the young boy wouldn't go down easy.

He got things in motion early and had someone deliver the kilos and paraphernalia to Shark to get him started. He had one of his young boys present in the projects with Shark to keep an eye on things.

It was plausible to Shark because he owed over $100,000. Psycho's true intentions, however, were to have eyes and ears on the operation. When the time came, Psycho could make his move with relative ease. It was a brilliant plan. He thought to himself, "*sinister*, but brilliant".

Chapter 26

Body woke at 6:30 am due to the movements of his cellmate. He couldn't rest in a strange place with strange people moving around. He had always been a light sleeper and the slightest movement would wake him. His cellmate hurried out of the cell and into the breakfast line. Body was a new intake, so he hadn't had an opportunity to order commissary. He hadn't eaten anything since the previous day and the hunger pangs were starting to kick in. He reluctantly got up and followed his bunky to the mess line. Luckily for him it was syrup day, which meant waffles or pancakes. Either one he figured couldn't be too bad. The inmate serving the trays recognized Body from the streets. He gave him an extra tray and attempted to make small talk.

Body wasn't sure where he knew the man from. But, it was too early to be listening to his bullshit. He accepted the extra tray and made his way back to his cell. The other inmates found their places at one of the tables scattered throughout the pod and ate their breakfast. Body preferred to eat in his room. He wasn't in the social mood, so he tried avoiding people.

He was placed on Pod 8D. It was the top floor of the sixteen story building. Each pod had two tiers. Most of the people housed there had serious charges like homicide, kidnapping and armed robbery.

After breakfast, the tier sanitation crew had to perform their morning chores, before all doors were put on *access* for recreation.

Access allowed the inmates to control their own doors. It was a safer policy than opening all the doors at once. As soon as Body stepped onto the tier, he heard the guard call his name. Both correctional officers working the morning shift were balding White men who looked to be in their late 60's. One was thin and sickly looking, like retirement should've happened fifteen years ago. The other was an obese man with a double chin and looked to be suffering from hypertension. The duo reminded him of the movie *Grumpy Old Men*.

"Jones! Lawyer visit!" said the sickly one.

"That's what I'm talking about!" Body exclaimed more to himself than anyone else.

It was 8:00 am in the morning and his lawyer was there bright and early. He smiled to himself as he headed through the sallyport, prepared to leave the pod.

"You got your ID with you?" asked the guard.

"Yeah, I got it!"

"Alright, go to the elevator and get off on the sixth floor. Make a right and there should be an officer at the desk there. They'll tell you the rest."

"Aight, I got it." said Body. He was anxious to hear what Aderman had to say.

Body got off the elevator on the sixth floor, made a right and approached the young female C.O. on post.

"What's up, Body?" said the guard with a smirk.

Body looked into her face and recognition flashed in his eyes, Meek Meek. Tameeka Greene was medium brown, 5'2" and slightly bow legged. Her hair was neatly manicured box braids hanging to the small of her back. It reminded him of Janet Jackson in *Poetic Justice*. Her legs were thick and her lips were desirable. A native of Pittsburgh's North Side. She always had a thing for Body.

"Oh shit! What's good, Meek?"

"Shit, just working and paying the bills."

"I hear that. I ain't know you worked down here." said Body.

"Yeah, I've been here almost a year now. I'll talk to you when you finish ya lawyer visit. He's in that room waiting for you." she said pointing him in the right direction.

Body stepped into the makeshift conference room where John Aderman stood to greet him.

"How's it going, Body?" he said using his nickname to greet him.

"You tell me, John."

"Well, it's still early and this was very short notice, so I don't have many details. But, you know I've got some sources. After a few well placed phone calls, I was able to gather that this is a first degree homicide charge. The probable cause is a *dying declaration*." said Aderman.

"A what?" he asked, incredulously.

"A dying declaration. It basically means that this guy who was shot supposedly gave a statement before dying. All the statement has to consist of is your name in order for the probable cause to exist. I know it sounds like a bunch of bullshit, but that's the way the system works." said Aderman.

"Man, this shit is fucked up! I don't even know this motherfucker they're accusing me of killing."

"Just calm down. I'll take care of it. We're scheduled to go for the coroner's inquest on Monday. We'll find out more then."

"What about my bail?" asked Body in hopes that he would be leaving jail one way or another. He would either post bond or be released after the preliminary hearing.

"We'll work on the bail, later. Let's get this inquest taken care of first. Now, I won't hold any punches with you kid. All the coroner's inquest is to determine whether there's sufficient evidence to proceed to trial. This guy isn't a judge and cannot determine the credibility of any witness. Basically, all a witness has to do is show up and the case will be held for trial."

"What witness could they possibly have? I didn't do the shit." said Body.

"Well, since it's a dying declaration, the statement had to be made to someone. In this case, it was a police officer. From what I know, the statements were made to homicide Detectives Richard Collins and John Novak. They'll testify that before Packard took his last breath, he identified you as his shooter. I'm familiar with these cops, Body. They're dirty. Won't play fair. But, don't worry 'cause if they put shit in the game, the gloves come off." said Aderman.

"Yeah, well I hope so. I don't like the sound of this shit."

"I understand your worries. Just let me handle this and we'll have you at home with that beautiful wife of yours in no time." he assured him.

At the mere mention of her, he felt saddened all over again. She was in her third trimester and Body wanted to be there for the birth of his first born child. He needed to be there. They still didn't know the sex. They wanted to be surprised. Secretly, he hoped for a boy.

After he shook hands with his attorney and thanked him for coming, he headed back to his pod. He passed by Tameeka on his way to the elevator without even acknowledging her. His head was in a daze. The look was written all over his face. When she noticed his demeanor, she didn't bother him. In her short tenure working at the jail she'd seen many inmates leave lawyer visits upset. She just picked up her walkie-talkie and called the control center for an elevator to send him back to his unit.

Chapter 27

Monday morning took forever to arrive. Body was up bright and early for the inquest. It was scheduled for 9am, so he had to be dressed and ready by 7. He was escorted to the elevator which he rode to the ground floor. It was the same intake bullpens where he was held his first night there. He was placed in a holding cell and given a brown paper bag containing his breakfast. It consisted of a styrofoam cup of Cheerios, three packets of sugar, a carton of milk and two slices of bread.

In the next forty five minutes, the bullpen became unbearably overcrowded. There was hardly any room to move. Finally, Body's name was called to appear before the judge. He was cuffed, shackled, led through the corridors and up a flight of stairs where he entered a courtroom. He looked around for familiar faces. Mila, Psycho and Taliban were seated in the front row. His attorney was finishing up a conversation with the judge and approached his client.

"Hey, how ya feeling?" asked Aderman, breaking the ice.

"Like shit! I'm just ready to get the ball rolling on this shit. The sooner this is over with the better." was Body's reply.

"Now listen. Here's what's gonna happen. These cops are gonna testify that they were given your name moments before the victim died. The judge will hold the case for trial. And once we're assigned a trial judge, I'll put in a bail motion." said Aderman.

"How long will all of this take?" asked Body.

"We'll have a pretrial conference within thirty days. We'll know who our trial judge will be and I'll have an opportunity to submit my motions. One of which will be a dismissal. I'm gonna get you out of here. We just have to let the process run its course. I'll have a discovery for you shortly." said Aderman.

The judge called for order in the court and gave a single bang of the gavel. The DA opened up about the severity of the case and the strength of the probable cause. When he finished, Detective Novak was the first of the two officers to approach the witness stand and be sworn in. The bailiff approached the detective holding a Holy Bible.

"Do you swear to tell the truth, the whole truth and nothing, but the truth. So help you, God?"

"I do!"

"Please state your name for the record, sir."

"Detective John Novak! N-O-V-A-K."

"Thank you. Detective, were you in the Garfield area on Fern Street on October 23rd?"

"Yes, I was."

"And did you receive a dispatch call to that area because shots were fired?"

"Yes, I did."

This is child's play, thought Body. The DA led the cop into every favorable answer he desired. Body was no lawyer, but he had watched enough *Law and Order* to know leading, when he heard it. The DA went through a series of setup questions. Then, got to the meat of the testimony.

"And did you have an opportunity to speak to the victim before he lost consciousness?"

"Yes, I did."

"And what, if anything, did he say to you, detective?"

"He said *Body* shot me."

"And did you have an idea of who this *Body* guy was?"

"Yes, I heard his name come up a time or two through previous investigations."

Man this pig is full of shit. Body could smell a set up from a mile away. The only question that remained was why were they out to get him. Something was telling him that it had to do with that *Frankstown Massacre.* Just the thought of it made him angry with Psycho. That was a stupid move that managed to gain national attention.

"So, what happened next, detective?"

"Since, I was familiar with the name Body. I asked the victim, if he meant it was Jabar Jones that shot him."

"And what was the reply, if any?"

"He said yes. Jabar Jones shot me."

It took a lot of self restraint for Body to keep his composure. He couldn't believe his ears. This whole thing sounded like a well rehearsed script.

Once the DA finished his line of questioning, John Aderman had an opportunity to cross examine the witness. He kept his cross examination brief, knowing how the preliminary stage worked. He wanted to save his ammo for the Superior Court in front of the trial judge. He would poke holes all through the state's case.

The next witness called to the stand was Detective Richard Collins. *Slave Catcher*, Body mumbled when he saw the detective. He was sworn in and taken through a similar line of questioning as his partner. This was done to corroborate the things Detective Novak said. The only other witness called to the stand was a medical examiner. His only purpose was to establish that a death had, in fact, occurred and the cause of the death was gunshot wounds to the upper torso. The medical examiner was an older man of Indian descent. His accent was very strong and his knowledge was very extensive. At times, he was asked to repeat himself by either the DA, defensive attorney or the stenographer.

Aderman had a rather important line of questioning for the medical examiner. The questions would potentially show inconsistencies in the detectives statements and reveal the fabrication, he was sure existed.

"Defense, your witness." said the Judge.
Aderman rose to his feet and slowly made his way toward the witness.

"Good morning, doctor. In your direct examination, you made mention of the location of the gunshot wounds. One being to the abdominal region and three to the upper torso. A total of four shots?"

"Correct." said the doctor with his accent apparent.

"I, also, heard you make mention of a lung collapse?"

"Correct."

"Would these wounds inflicted by the gunshot, in your professional opinion, cause a tremendous amount of blood loss?"

"Yes. The victim suffered immeasurable amounts of blood loss."

"With those kinds of injuries and the significant amount of blood loss sustained, in your professional opinion, how long would the victim have to remain conscious?"

"Maybe, sixty seconds." That was the response given by a highly educated and recommended doctor.

Now, Body was gaining a better understanding of what Aderman was attempting to establish with his questioning. If the victim only had sixty seconds of consciousness, there was no way the detectives could have extracted that statement from him. If they arrived on the scene ten or twelve minutes after the shooting, as the police reports suggest, that would be contrary to science. Body smiled to himself. He knew his lawyer was thorough. He would dismantle the case like he promised. It just sucked to have to play the waiting game while he remained in custody. It was time to check up on that bail situation, again.

Chapter 28

Months passed since Body's incarceration and Psycho had managed to maintain the lucrative operation in his absence. Body became the consigliere and advised his man to success. He relayed all information concerning the shipments through visits. Neither of them trusted any phones. They didn't even trust the phones used for the standard non-contact visits. Psycho would attend lawyer visits as an assistant of Aderman to discuss business with him. Body had one main request for the moment, *no war.*

Psycho enjoyed the war aspect more than hustling and felt a tremendous amount of power whenever he could eliminate a foe. *Checkmate.* It was like a chess match to him and he wanted to *"out chess"* all his opponents, including the ones who weren't aware that they were opponents. They would go down the easiest.

Psycho was driving down Perrysville Ave on the North Side. He flipped open his trap phone and placed a call.

"Yo!" answered Shark.

"What's good, Ike? I'm close to you. So, be ready." said Psycho.

"I'm always ready to get his paper, Cuz."

"I'll see you in five minutes."

Psycho ended the call and continued to bop his head to the music. Just as he suspected, a new way of packaging the coke, a purer product, and a different method of cooking it up. The cash flow through Northview Heights had skyrocketed. Shark was now moving over one and a half kilos of crack daily. The vials were filled to maximum capacity which was preferable to the fiends. Psycho used a minimal amount of cut on the product. Just like Body showed him. Then, he would put the correct ratio of peppermints into the pyrex. He was branding his coke differently from everyone else's. It was the recipe that deserved the credit for Northview's success.

He was on his way to meet with Shark and Stickman. He was left behind and tasked with watching over the operation and reporting on Shark. As Psycho pulled into the projects, he noticed how busy it was. He spotted Shark and Stickman standing in front of Shark's new white 760Li BMW. *Stepping his game all the way up,* thought Psycho. A slight grin creased his face.

He rolled down the window to address the men.

"I see you stepping up your game. That's what I like to see. We 'bout to have you up this bitch in a Bentley." He gassed Shark and said, "Get in."

The duo approached the Durango and Stickman jumped in the back seat allowing Shark to ride shotgun.

"What's crackin', Cuz?" said Shark as he got adjusted in his seat.

"You, Big Money. I got something real special for you being as though you've stepped ya game up, so quick. I'm ready to take you to the next level." Psycho stroked his ego as he pulled away from the curb. Shark's face reflected his enthusiasm. His eyes sparkled with dollar signs.

"I'm about to make you a part of the family. Officially." said Psycho, *baking the cake.*

"Instead of me bringing the keys to you, I'm showing you the spot. So, you can send one of ya trusted people through to pick up for you. I got twenty birds on stand still for you right now."

"That's what the fuck I'm talking bout!" exclaimed Shark.

Stickman passed him a blunt stuffed with sour diesel in an effort to keep him relaxed. Shark graciously accepted the blunt feeling the love he was shown.

"Ya'll know how to treat a nigga." said Shark in between tokes of the potent marijuana.

Psycho turned up the volume on the system and Jay-Z's voice came blaring through the speakers:

"Niggas will show you love that's how they fool thugs. Before you know it, you lying in a pool of blood. Cough up a lung where I'm from... Marcy son... Ain't nothing nice... "

Psycho sang along to the lyrics and Shark was none the wiser. His spider senses hadn't tingled and alerted him of danger. He never noticed Psycho cutting his eyes in his direction while he sang the deceptive lyrics. Psycho was driving down the parkway headed for Butler County.

Thirty five minutes later, he pulled up to an old building and killed the engine. All three men exited the truck and made their way inside.

"Damn cuz, what type of building is this shit?" asked Shark.

Psycho just smiled, not caring to answer Shark's inquiry. He was ahead of the pack, leading the way. Stickman was bringing up the rear. He walked through a set of stainless steel doors. Shark followed a few paces behind. His mind was racing with all sorts of expectations. He knew that Psycho and his crew were getting money and had heard stories. He had this vision in his mind that he would walk through the doors and come face to face with stacks of kilos. Enough coke to fill an olympic size swimming pool, like he saw in those documentaries. He followed behind Psycho with sweaty palms of nervous anticipation. When Shark walked through the brightly lit room, he felt a sudden sense of pain register to his brain before everything went black.

What could've happened, he thought. Did some kilos fall on my head, he wondered. Did somebody hit me with something?

He stirred awake a short while later with a thunderous headache. His vision was impaired and the three figures that stood before him were blurry. Slowly, things came back into focus and he regained his sight. The first thing he noticed was that he had been tied up, bound at the hands and feet, lying on what he assumed to be a rusty table. He quickly looked towards the three men. There was Psycho, Stickman and some guy that he didn't recognize holding a small blackjack that was probably the cause of his headache. It looked to be police issued.

Damn, cuz must've knocked me out with that shit, thought Shark. He was trying to wrap his mind around what he could've done to make the plug come at him like this. He was running up numbers on the block. Stickman's present was of no surprise to him. He was just a runner and

207

Shark never trusted him. Something about him said snake and he never wanted him around. He only tolerated him because of Body and Psycho.

Taliban stood in the corner of the room wearing a sinister smile. He thought he could read Shark's mind. He imagined that Shark wondered who he was and if he hit him with the blackjack.

"Fuck is going on, Cuz?" Shark managed to ask.

"What's going on Shark, my nigga, is that your time in the game has expired." said Psycho. He was toying with some sort of machinery, but Shark couldn't tell what it was.

"Fuck is you talking 'bout, Cuz? I thought we was family now. Fuck happened to that?" said Shark in an angry and hurt tone.

"We are family... us right here." said Psycho referring to Taliban, Stickman, and himself.

"Unfortunately, there's no room for anyone else. I know you're a bit confused. So, let me at least clarify some shit for you. You didn't wanna accept the first offer we gave you to split the block which would've kept you around. Now, we'll keep the whole thing for ourselves. You gotta go. It's a shame, too, cause I actually liked you."

"Fuck you, pussy!" spat Shark.

"See, that's why I like you, Shark. You got balls. But, it's the same reason I gotta kill you first. Sooner or later it would've come down to either you or me."

"You's a grimy ass nigga, Cuz! Fuck you, Stick! You fag ass nigga!"

Shark elevated his head from the table and spat in Stickman's face. Stickman, instantly, became furious and pulled his glock .17 from his waistband and aimed it at Shark's head. Psycho intervened, before it could go any further. He had his own plan for how things would play out.

"Nah, Stick. At first, I was gonna shoot this nigga in the head, too. I wanted to get this shit over with quick. It was gonna be a gift to this nigga, but since he like to spit in nigga's faces, he's 'bout to be punished."

"Fuck you, nigga! Fuck I'm supposed to be scared? I'll see you niggas in hell!" yelled Shark.

He always said when the time came, he would go out like a G. To him that meant being unwilling to give his captors the satisfaction of seeing him cry, beg or plead for his life. As soon as the realization set in that he was going to die, he made his decision to do it like a man. It was a decision, he would soon regret. He would no longer be receiving the shot to the head, he was so sure was coming. That would be too kind for a man who spat in the face of Psycho or his crew.

"Yeah, you gonna see us in hell, alright." said Psycho.

He pulled a lever and opened the door of hell. A dangerous gust of heat escaped and a roaring sound of a blazing fire inside. When Shark realized what Psycho had in store for him, he felt a rush of fear that he's never experienced in his life and he lost control of his bowels. He soiled his boxers and jeans and began to futilely struggle against his restraints.

"Unfortunately for you, you'll be experiencing the depths of hell a lot sooner than any of us!" he said.

He gave Shark a hard push and watched as he was consumed by the fire head first. If you listened closely, you could hear his skin sizzling. If you breathed, you smelt his burnt flesh. His screams came from the pit of his stomach. Stickman couldn't stomach it any longer and he slammed the machine door shut. A sickening smell lingered in the air.

***

Although, Body was still confined to jail, his spirits were as high as ever. Things were beginning to look up for him. It was a new year and Mila had given birth to a beautiful, baby girl named Isabella. She weighed in at 7lbs 8oz and had thick curly hair. Body was secretly hoping for a boy, but he was just as ecstatic to have his baby girl. She was his little princess.

To put the icing on the cake, America was preparing for the Inauguration of its first Black President. Everyone was excited about all the possibilities the future may bring. Body felt a sense of pride knowing a Black man had won and would officially take over the White House. It made him feel like anything was possible. He was the tier representative for his pod and he demanded the right to vote for all those who were eligible. He found out that he wasn't precluded from voting because he hadn't been convicted and was awaiting trial. Naturally, he wanted the same thing for the rest of the inmate population who were eligible as well. He was a part of the Obama victory and it felt damn good.

When he watched the Inauguration on TV, he knew that once he left jail, he wasn't going back to the same life he once lived. He had been juggling the idea of moving away from Pittsburgh to make his transition from the game easier. He knew that the situation he was in would only be the beginning of bad things to come, if he stayed. He could afford to disappear. So, he would.

The two detectives, Greasy & Grimy, paid him a visit offering to make his problems go away, if he could provide information about *The Frankstown Massacre*. He had the feeling all along that is what everything boiled down to. Now that he had confirmation, he knew it would only get worse. He was G coded. He would adhere to the laws of the streets. He told both detectives, "Fuck you bacon smelling motherfuckers! I'm outta here," as he stormed out of the room.

He already received his discovery material by that point. He knew the state's entire case amounted to nothing. He felt pretty confident for a man fighting for his life.

In a last-ditch effort to make sure the case stuck and Body continued to sit in jail, the detectives fabricated more evidence. This time it was a statement from a mysterious eye witness who identified Body via photo array.

Body was nervous that the setup may be a little deeper than he imagined. Aderman quickly helped him to put those thoughts to rest. The statement from the alleged witness had no signature at the bottom which indicated that nobody adopted the statement as their own. However, this was a bail hearing and not a trial. The evidence was to be deemed credible for the proceedings, cried the assistant DA. He would play possum like he had an eye witness and ask for denial of bail. In the Commonwealth of Pennsylvania, if you are charged with a crime that is punishable by death or life imprisonment, you can be denied bail. If you had The Honorable Judge Henry Hacken presiding over your case, you would be denied.

He was secretly referred to as "Cracken Hacken" because he was known to crack a brotha in the head in his courtroom. There was a legend of how he once sentenced a defendant. He had him count the pigeons on the massive ledge. The defendant peered out of the window and answered with thirty seven. The judge then sentenced him to thirty seven years. The sentencing may not have been the best time to start being honest.

In spite of all the adversity, Body felt good and thought ultimately he was winning. Yeah, he was incarcerated for the moment, but he knew it was momentary. He had his beautiful baby girl, a Black President, and he received the news that Robin successfully completed rehab. She was doing well, attending frequent Narcotic Anonymous meetings and keeping contact with her sponsor for support. Body was proud of his raise and he could tell that this year would be a good one. He smiled at the thought, then turned up the volume on the Sony walkman that he purchased from commissary. It wasn't anything fancy. It only played local radio stations, so he settled on WAMO 100.1. The raspy voice of Young Jeezy's song "My President" came blaring through the headphones. Body sang along, proudly:

"My President is Black. My Lambo's blue. And I'll be goddamned, if my rims aint too. My mama ain't home and my daddy still in jail...Anybody seen the scale?"

***

Body managed to make his stay in the county a rather comfortable one. He pulled strings to get himself a single-man cell, so he wouldn't be forced to deal with anyone he didn't want to. He ate like a king in jail. The things that society considered normal like some fast food or a home cooked meal were of the highest delicacy in jail, right after pussy and drugs. If you were able to have sex with a correctional officer, nurse, teacher, or any other willing woman, it trumped anything else you could possibly conjure up. Body had each of the big three. He smoked weed like he had his own grow operation. He ate well and he was fucking Tameeka. He liked her a lot. She was pretty. Her lips were full and her hips were wide. She was petite, but her body was curvy. She was smart and working on a degree in Criminal Justice at Duquesne University with plans to leave her C.O. profession. Had it not been for Mila, she could've been his wifey. He knew she was a good catch. Most of the girls her age already had multiple children, some by multiple men. Tameeka didn't have any.

Old feelings were rekindled after seeing each other and having a few conversations. She would call his unit and have him sent to consultation even when his lawyer wasn't there. Just to kick it. She was aware of his relationship with Mila, but convinced herself that she was more than capable of having a platonic friendship with him. Not before long, her protective walls caved and she became overwhelmed by a flood of emotions. Every time she saw him, her eyes sparkled, her heart fluttered and pussy moistened in lust. It had been nineteen months since her last sexual encounter, so she was in heat. A bid opened up to become a full time officer on the pod where Body was housed and she knew immediately that she wanted it. It would give her an opportunity to see him five days a week. She made the sacrifice. She switched shifts.

She talked to him throughout the nights on the cell phone she had given him. She engaged him in stimulating conversations. He had consumed her thoughts. He had to be very discreet with the phone. *No one knew it existed.* Having it made life and business a lot easier for him. He could call directly to the streets and keep up with the organization and his money. Plus, it beat using a jail phone, where all calls are subject to monitoring and recording.

Body wanted to check up on his man from Northview Projects. Last he had heard, the 'jects were doing very well and his man upgraded his BMW. It had been a minute since they last spoke. He tried to make contact a few times and each attempt sent him to a full mailbox. He figured he must've gotten a new number or new phone. Psycho hadn't heard from him. If he were in jail, Body would've known because he was already there. And if he had gotten spanked, the streets would've been buzzing with that information. He knew just who to call to get some clarity on the situation.

"Yo!" he answered.

"Leroy?"

"Yeah, who's this?"

"This is Body. What's good, Ike?"

"Oh shit. What's crackin', Cuz? When you come home?"

"Nah, my nigga. I'm not home, yet. But, I'll be there soon. I just got my hands on a jack. That's all."

"Oh, aight. So, what's good?"

"Listen, I'm trying to get in touch with Shark, but his phone is off."

"Shark?" asked Leroy.

"Yeah nigga, Shark!"

Leroy and Shark were first cousins. Leroy was a small time hustler from the Northside who Shark would give packages to keep money in his pockets. It was well known that Leroy was under Shark's wing even though he was seven years older than him. You could often catch him driving Shark's car, stunting for unsuspecting women at the club.

"Man, ain't nobody seen Shark in months! It's like the nigga disappeared off the face of the earth."

"Fuck you mean, he disappeared?" asked Body.

"I mean he disappeared! Stopped answering his phone. Copped a brand new 760Li BMW that was sitting in the projects for months, just collecting dust. I'm trying to get my aunt to give up the keys. His baby mama, kids, or his raise haven't seen him. At first my aunt and them thought he went to jail or something. They called around everywhere. Even all the hospitals and morgues in all the surrounding counties. That nigga's nowhere to be found. I think that nigga might've had warrants and shit."

"Aight, if he turns up give him this number." said Body.

"I don't think he's gonna show up, Cuz. Ya man, Psycho and his people run the whole projects now. Got that shit locked down."

215

Chapter 29

When Body ended the call, his mind began racing with thoughts. Sitting around in the county jail, you would hear all the rumors from the streets. Sometimes, you hear about things in the county faster than people hear about them on the streets. Body had heard of other people coming up missing around the city. He even heard a few names he knew. But, he dismissed it as jailhouse gossip. But now, it was starting to look like that gossip may have more validity than he was willing to give it. He would have to investigate some more.

For now, he would concentrate on his trial date which was scheduled for June 11th, right before the beginning of summer. Aderman warned him that it was difficult to get a jury in the summer. But, he would do everything he could to get the case pushed forward. He also teetered the line of guaranteeing his client an outcome. Aderman was convinced that the case wouldn't stand in trial because it had no legs to stand on. Body was super excited at the prospect of going home for the summer. He shared the news with Tameeka. She was ecstatic for him.

She had her mind set on locking Body down. She had made moves for him that she would never do for anyone. She put her entire career on the line for him. She brought in weed, cellphones, and the kind of home cooked food that was sure to get to his heart. She never figured she had the nerve. On Saturdays, usually her day off, she worked overtime stationed at her old post on the 6th floor calling inmates for lawyer visits. Administration wasn't present in the building during the weekends and everything was more relaxed.

Tameeka looked at the logbook and noticed there weren't any consultations scheduled for the next forty five minutes. She picked up the phone and called to the eighth floor.

"Jones! Lawyer visit!" yelled the guard.

Body wasn't expecting Aderman to show up. *It better be good news*, he thought as he headed through the sallyport and off the pod. His mind was racing with thoughts. He tried to imagine what news his lawyer may have. He got off the elevator on the sixth floor and was shocked to see Tameeka working.

"What are you doing here? I thought you had the day off."

"I did. Overtime."

"Is my lawyer here or did you call me down here to talk, 'cause you're bored?"

"No, your lawyer isn't here. As a matter of fact, nobody's lawyer will be here for," She paused and looked at her watch for emphasis, " thirty five more minutes. I wanna show you something real quick." she said.

She rose from her seat and led the way into the gymnasium. It was the only gym where the men could play full court basketball. It was known as "The Big Gym". The entrance was located behind the guard's stationary desk. It was used throughout the week for recreation and every Friday for Jummah.

She entered the gym, made a left and walked toward the rear with Body following closely behind. He admired her ass in the tight fitting, navy uniform. His interest was piqued when she opened the door to the inmate bathroom and went inside. As soon as he entered the bathroom, she was all over him. Kissing him passionately, running her hands all over his toned frame and squeezing the bulge that was begging for attention. He matched her passion as he returned her kiss and squeezed her ass. Both of their hormones were raging from the deprivation. She let her hands roam freely, tugging at the manhood trapped inside his pants. The red, county issued uniform had an elastic waistband. They came down with one firm tug. She grabbed his manhood in her small manicured hand and it began to stiffen in her clutch. She felt it throbbing and getting harder by the second. She squatted and hungrily shoved him into her mouth. His toes curled from the sensation. He grabbed the back of Tameeka's head and stroked her mouth. Tameeka didn't flinch. She accepted his thrusts and deep-throated him with an expertise that would make Super Head blush.

Body couldn't take it any longer. He was standing on his tiptoes. He pulled her up to her feet and unfastened her pants. He got more excited at the sight of her turquoise silk panties. The panty liner she wore failed to hide her excitement. He nearly lost control at the sight of the wet stain in the middle of her silk panty. He squatted down and removed the ACG boot from her left foot without caring to untie it, first. Tameeka wiggled her leg out of her pants and panty. He firmly spun her around, bent her over the sink and penetrated her deep. A gasp escaped her lips as he filled her completely. She had one hand secured on the wall. She used the other hand to hold onto the side of the sink while he stroked her with powerful thrusts. Everything about this seemed right to Tameeka. *It was spontaneous, dangerous, risky and exciting.* Just the thought was enough to make her cum, again. It didn't hurt that she was in love with Body. It made the sex much better for her. He grunted out sounds of pleasure as he pounded Tameeka's tight, wet pussy. The sound of sweaty skin slapping together echoed in the small bathroom. The sound her wet pussy made was like stirring macaroni and cheese. He tried to hold on for just a moment longer as his dick mushroomed. He exploded, letting his seed escape deep inside her.

They were panting and damp with perspiration. Tameeka used a wet paper towel to clean herself and then Body. She looked at her watch and knew they should hurry. She quickly dressed and sent Body back to his pod feeling like the luckiest man in the world.

<u>***</u>

In the months that followed, Psycho's reign in the city grew more powerful. He managed to bring a reign of terror that the city of Pittsburgh had never seen before. Hustlers were afraid like never before. The scariest thing for them wasn't that people were being killed, but the fact that so many people were missing without a trace and nobody knew exactly what happened to them. As the speculations and rumors swirled, Psycho decided that he would set an example once and for all to let motherfuckas know who was really running the city. *And* it wasn't the fucking Mayor. That was his weakness, he never knew when enough was enough. He called a meeting between his most trusted lieutenants, Taliban and Stickman. ManMan wasn't there because he was sent upstate for a violation of probation.

The official business at hand was orchestrating a hit on Big Rome. The man who had control over the Hazelwood section of the city. He was respected for his fair treatment of his people and being a gentle giant. Big Rome was 6' 4", 265 lbs. He was no push-over, just as vicious as he was humble. He had been working very closely with Stickman all year long. The two had become good friends. Big Rome oversaw the entire Hazelwood operation from a house on Elizabeth Street. It was a lucrative setup to say the least.

"I wanna send a clear message this time." said Psycho. The look in his eyes was inexplicable.

"I want ya'll to stop at *Home Depot* and cop a chainsaw. We gonna chop this big muthafucka down to size!" he said in a demonic tone.

They knew Psycho well enough to know that he meant business when he had that look in his eyes. Taliban didn't give a fuck. Psycho was his man. They were brothers and he was game for anything. Stickman, however, felt different. He didn't want any part of the plan and it registered on his face.

"Fuck, you gotta a problem with this shit, Stick?" asked Psycho in an authoritative tone.

"Nah, man. I'm good." he lied. He started to object, but changed his mind. He knew better than to challenge Psycho.

"Good. I know you helped bake a couple cakes, but I hope you're ready to put in some real work." said Psycho.

Stickman knew in his gut that he was about to be asked to do something he couldn't do. *This nigga always coming up with some crazy shit*, he thought. He reluctantly replied, "Yeah, I'm ready."

Psycho was pleased and he adjourned the meeting. Stickman offered to go out and purchase the chainsaw. What he really wanted was to get as far away from Psycho as possible. He refused to take part in the hit on Rome. Furthermore, he refused to be hacking up anybody with a chainsaw. He was sure Psycho would make him do it.

"Crazy muthafucka!" Stickman spat underneath his breath as he got into his car. He couldn't just tell Psycho that he wasn't gonna participate. There wasn't any telling what he might do. At that instant, he knew what it was he had to do.

He flipped open his cell phone and began scrolling down his call log in search of Big Rome's number. He quickly located the number then paused.

"*On second thought,*" he said to himself. He pressed the clear button and dialed another number. After three rings a man picked up.

"Homicide Division, Detective Novak here."
Stickman's armpits began to sweat and his palms were clammy. He almost couldn't believe what he was about to do. He sat on the phone for a second, contemplating.

"Hello, anybody there?"
Stickman swallowed the lump in his throat.

"Yeah, I'm here."

"How can I help you?"

"You still interested in *The Frankstown Massacre?*"

With the mention of the biggest case in the history of the city and the thought of possibly gaining information to crack the case open, Detective Novak sprang to his feet in an excited rush. At the mere prospect of solving the case, caused the detective's palms to sweat and the small prick inside his trousers to stiffen.

"Yeah, I'm interested." he said in an attempt to hide his excitement.

"Well, I can give you all the information you need for the case. I know all the shooters *and* why they did it *and* who planned it. But, I need immunity and I wanna be relocated."

"What's your involvement?" asked the detective, while feverishly scribbling on a notepad.

"I was the driver."

"That's it?"

"That's it."

"I can protect you from prosecution, definitely. *And* have you relocated, immediately after the trial. But, you have to turn yourself over to me. *So, I can protect you.* What's your name?"

"My name is Mario Steward. They call me Stickman."

After Stickman wrapped up his call with the detective, he felt a twinge of guilt. But, what was done was done. He knew he couldn't kill Psycho and Taliban. So, the next best thing was to put them in jail, where they couldn't hurt him or anyone else. Body was already in jail for a homicide, so he wouldn't have to worry about him either. He knew it was difficult to beat a homicide charge and from what he heard there were some police testifying on him.

Yeah, Body's finished too, he convinced himself without any facts. The only one left to worry about was Man Man, but he would make sure he never came home from his short term bid upstate. He would tell on Man Man, too.

Chapter 30

Body sat in his cell reading. That's how he often passed the time. He was reading a lot of the books that Mama Jones sent him. He read books by Fred Hampton, Geronimo Pratt, Mumia Abu Jamal, and George Jackson. He was so impressed with George's book "Soledad Brothers", that he wanted to share what he learned with his grandraise. On a visit, he was able to recite some of the book. He was attempting to get an old lady to adopt new views. As he sat in his cell, he reminisced about a particular visits.

"Listen to this grandma: *The American Buffalo, he's a herd animal or social animal, if you prefer. Just like us in that matter. We're social animals. We need others of our general kind around us to feel secure. Few men would enjoy total isolation. The buffalo, cattle and some others are like people in the aspect that they need company most of the time.*

Of all the world's people, we, Blacks love the company of others, most. We are the most socialistic. Social animals eat, sleep, and travel with company. They need this company to feel secure. This fact means that socialistic animals, also, need leaders. It follows logically that if the buffalo is going to eat, sleep, and travel in groups; some coordinating factors are needed or some will be sleeping, when others are traveling.

Predatory men learned of the natural occurrence of leadership in all social animals. That each group will by nature, produce a leader. And to these leaders falls the responsibility for organizing them for survival. The buffalo hunter knew

223

that if he could isolate and identify the leader and kill him first, the rest of the herd would be helpless; at his mercy, to be killed off as he saw fit.

We Blacks have the same problem the buffalo had. We have the same weaknesses, also, and the predatory man understands this weakness, well. Medgar Evers, Malcolm X, Bobby Hutton, Featherstone, W.L. Noland, M.L. King, Mark Clark, and Fred Hampton, just a few who have already gone by way of the buffalo."

He could remember the first time he read that. He just closed the book. Sat back for a while and daydreamed about being a revolutionary back in those times. His thoughts were interrupted by the vibrating of his cell phone.

He looked at the caller ID and smiled as he answered the phone.

"Damn, girl! You couldn't wait to get in here to see me, huh?" He didn't even give Tameeka time to say hello, before he started to tease her.

"Hey, Papi. Yeah, I miss you. But, that's not why I'm calling. I'm calling to tell you that ya boys just got knocked".

"What?" he asked in a confused manner.

"Ya boy, Psycho. They arrested him and the other one. Turn on the news."

Body quickly ended the call without responding. He ran out of his cell and went straight to the common area, where half the inmates on the tier were crowded in front of the TV watching 50 cent's new music video. Body grabbed the remote off the C.O.'s desk and changed the channel to the news. At the abrupt changing of channels and no warning, everyone turned their attention in Body's direction. Everyone was aware of who he was and decided to avoid confrontation with him. Body raised the volume and watched the broadcast in disbelief.

"We're here in front of the Sheriff building where two men are being held in connection with The Frankstown Massacre. That's the mass shooting that left five men dead and six others seriously injured. The Massacre occurred during a funeral on Frankstown Road. Police have been searching high and low for any clues or information that would crack this case open. Leading Homicide Detectives in the investigation received information via a confidential informant. This informant, my sources tell me, turns out to have been a participant in the mass attack. Exactly what role this informant played has not yet been revealed. The two suspects have been identified as 19 year old Raymond "Psycho" Brown and 18 year old David "Taliban" Marshal. Motives are being listed as an ongoing drug war and Raymond "Psycho" Brown is said to be a major player and distributor in the Pittsburgh drug trade."

Body couldn't believe his eyes and ears. *How the fuck did they get caught?* He wondered. He had a feeling that shit would one day hit the fan. He never imagined it would happen so quickly. It was fucked up that he was on his way out of jail and his man was on his way in. *Who the fuck is the snitch?* He wondered. He reflected back on the conversation he had with Psycho when he assured Body that nobody outside the crew knew about what took place. Body continued to watch the rest of the broadcast in shock.

"Authorities say that a third man, 21 year old Allen "Man Man" Greer, who is currently in prison on unrelated charges will face these charges as well..."

225

Damn, they got Man Man, too. Body thought. He was only serving a 1-2 year bid for submitting a dirty urine to his P.O. Now, he would be feeling the wrath, too. *At least they don't have Stickman,* thought Body. Little did he know, the police did have Stickman. They had him in protective custody.

<u>Chapter 31</u>

In the next few days that followed, the reports of the arrests made national news. Body was worried about word getting back to Jesus about their troubles. He knew that making national news couldn't be good for business. He found out that Psycho and Taliban were housed on 7D directly beneath Body's pod. The only way they were able to communicate with each other was by talking through the bowl. The bowl was a tactic routinely used by inmates to communicate throughout the jail. They would clear all the water out of their toilets and talk to other inmates connected to the same plumbing line.

A couple days after the news broadcast, Man Man was transferred to the county jail and placed on 8D with Body. Man Man, however, couldn't provide any information because he hadn't found out anything, yet himself. He was just as shocked as Body .

Body pulled some strings with Tameeka to have Psycho and Taliban moved to Pod 8D. They all embraced each other then everyone went into Body's cell to discuss the case. Man Man and Body were appalled to learn that Stickman was the rat eating the cheese.

"That rat ass nigga got us fucked up!"

"That's crazy. That nigga flipped like that. Da fuck he do that for?" said Man Man.

"Man, fuck that rat ass nigga!" spat Psycho and Taliban simultaneously.

"What ya'll lawyers talking about?" asked Body.

"Man, that shit don't look good, Ike." said Taliban.

"My mouthpiece said, if this nigga come to trial and snitch, basically, we can cancel Christmas. He made that determination without even having discovery. He got his hands on a police report and said this nigga, Stick, told them what kind of guns was used, how he got rid of the car and everything."

"Yeah. It's gonna be tough to beat this shit. That bitch ass nigga folded and brought down a dynasty." said Psycho.

"We need a way to touch that nigga." said Man Man.

"Man, that nigga is somewhere laid up in witness protection. How the fuck we gonna touch him?" asked Psycho.

"There's only one person I know with that kind of power." responded Body.

Suddenly, a light went off in his head. He had an idea. He went to his stash spot and retrieved his cell phone. He frantically began to dial a number from his mental rolodex. After a few rings, a man answered with a thick accent.

"Hello?"

"Hello, Juan? This is Body. I need to speak to Jesus asap!"

He exchanged knowing glances with Psycho and no words were necessary. They both knew that if anyone was able to lend some assistance, it would be Jesus Valencia, their connect.

"Body! What can I do for you, my friend?" came the cheerful voice of Jesus.

He went on in detail to explain his situation to Jesus. He spared no details, including the one about not being able to pay him his $3.2 million owed for the last consignment. He assured Jesus that he would get his money as soon as he could work out the details on how to get it to him. The entire call took twelve minutes and it was settled.

"What'd he say?" asked Psycho inquisitively. Body hadn't even press the end button before the questions began.

Jesus Valencia was a powerful man, who had the means to accomplish things most men couldn't. After receiving the phone call from Body, he weighed his options. On one hand, he could say fuck that nigger, he's on his own. He could terminate all contact with him and his partner. On the other hand, he would be losing out on his $3.2 million as well as immeasurable amounts of future cash flow. Plus, there was the fact that Body was the father of his granddaughter. Then there was also the likelihood that the snitch inside their circle had information that would affect his operations and somehow implicate him. With all things considered, it was an easy decision for Jesus to make. He would send one of his most trusted soldiers to exterminate the rat.

"He said not to worry about it. Said something about seeing a familiar face soon and everything will be taken care of. Whatever, that means. I just hope that he comes through for a nigga."

***

Everyone was lost in thought for a moment. They were flabbergasted that they would receive help from the *real* cartel. It was like a movie. They began to discuss the possibilities. Everyone felt a glimmer of hope after Body's last call. However, they still remained nervous and rightfully so. If they lost at trial, they would surely receive the death penalty. They had the city's number one district attorney, Mark Trolly, overseeing the case. The state was pulling all stops to make sure they received a conviction. Stickman had even received his $50,000 cash reward, prematurely. He had his mother and grandmother relocated down south, somewhere in Texas. He was under 24 hour surveillance, holed up in a Holiday Inn outside the city in Allentown, PA.

They talked about all the possible outcomes when they heard the guard yell.

"Jones! Lawyer visit!"

"Oh shit! That's Aderman. Let me go see what's up." said Body.

He grabbed his inmate ID and headed toward sallyport. He knew the routine well by this point. His lawyer was seated inside the attorney/client visiting room when Body walked in. He stood to greet Body as usual. This time he was wearing an oversized smile that told Body he came bearing good news.

"John, what's up? Tell me something good." he exclaimed. It was difficult for him to hide his excitement.

"How's this for good? I filed the motion for dismissal and the judge is gonna accept it, if the state doesn't produce this mysterious eye witness." said Aderman beaming with a smile.

"We're scheduled to go Monday. Same as planned, but this thing has no legs to stand on and it won't go to trial. I knew those fuckers whole plan was to keep you sitting in this hell hole as long as possible in hopes that you would break. What they really wanted was some info about that Massacre thing. Now that they've brought those guys in, nobody's thinking about you and the DA is folding his hand."

"That's great news!" exclaimed Body, matching Aderman's smile. His smile faded when he thought about the situation his team found themselves in.

"Just to be sure that you're out of here. I submitted a motion for a speedy trial. Those fuckers try violating your sixth amendment right and I'll grind their asses up in civil court."

This was the best news that Body could've hoped for. He had to end his visit with Aderman because it was shift change and he had to return to his pod for count. He was feeling alive and it was evident through the pep in his step.

He swaggered back to his pod anxious to share the news with Tameeka who should be there any minute. He didn't want to share it with his team just yet because he knew his excitement would shine through and he was empathetic towards their situation. He didn't want it highlighted that their misfortune was his blessing. It just wouldn't go over well.

He locked in his cell during the count and five minutes later he heard the click of his lock. He knew Tameeka was there and she probably wanted to see him. He walked towards the guards desk beaming.

He looked at her pretty face, which had its own glow. Her co-worker hadn't shown up yet, so they had an opportunity to talk in private.

"What's up, Ms. Green?" said Body, wearing his signature smile.

"Oh, it's Ms. Green now, huh?" she said playfully.

"Nah, what's up, Baby? I got some good news today and I wanted to share it with you."

"I got some good news today, too. You go first. I wanna save mine til' last." She said wearing a smile as pretty and bright as Body had ever seen it.

"I had a lawyer visit, today, a real one." He said with a wink. "It turns out that by Monday, I'll be going home."

"That's great news! It actually makes my news even better." exclaimed Tameeka.

"What happened?" Body asked, anxious to hear her good news, as well.

"Well, at first I wasn't sure, but I've been feeling a lil' queasy lately among other things. So, I went to check some things out… and… I'm pregnant! We're gonna have a baby!" she said reaching across the desk and placing her hand on the back of his hand.

The news hit Body like a sledgehammer. It was the last thing, he was expecting to hear and the furthest thing from his mind. Of course, he knew the possibilities of what could happen having unprotected sex. But, he just somehow figured it wouldn't happen. Thinking with his little head, he went to the big gym every Saturday and punished Tameeka inside the bathroom. Now, the reality of what he had been doing was hitting him full-force. His facial expressions changed, subconsciously, as he thought about what this could mean for his future. Tameeka picked up on his vibe and became concerned.

"What's wrong? You're not happy?"

"I'm not sure." he answered, truthfully.

"Oh, you're not sure? But you was sure to cum inside of me every time though, huh?" she said with a hint of attitude mixed with sorrow.

"You know it ain't even like that, Baby. It's just so unexpected. That's all." said Body in an attempt to soothe her feelings.

"Yeah, well you gotta expect that when you're having unprotected sex on a regular basis." she stated in a serious tone.

Before, they could delve any deeper into their conversation, Officer Scott walked onto the pod. He was Tameeka's partner. Body ended the conversation with her. He promised to discuss it further, later.

He went to his cell, where he laid back on his bunk staring up at the ceiling. His mind was congested with so many different thoughts and emotions. *Damn*, he thought. He had already been making arrangements to move away from the city. Mila had even gone to Atlanta to purchase them a nice home in the Buckhead section of the city. His mind was already set. He was getting away from the madness. He had yet to discuss his plans with anyone outside of his immediate family. He wasn't sure how his team would take the news, especially in light of their situation. But, Body had to make the best decision for himself and his family.

He was getting older and could no longer live for his crew. His birthday was only a couple weeks away and he wanted to live to see 21. He wanted to see it from the streets as opposed to the confinements of jail.

He hadn't broken the news to Tameeka concerning his move out of town. Now, with the news she laid on him it would be much more difficult to tell her. He could tell that she had her heart set on having this baby. He played with the idea of telling her to have an abortion. *Nah*, he thought, *she definitely ain't going for that.* Whatever he was gonna do, he would have to do it soon. After this weekend, he was leaving the city and wasn't looking back.

Chapter 32

Over the weekend, Body spent the majority of his time kicking it with his team. He didn't do any reading because he wanted to build with his people as much as he could. He was hopeful, but he wasn't sure when or if they would ever physically be together, again.

Body finally broke down and told everybody about his plans. Psycho took the news the hardest and felt like Body was running out on him. Man Man understood Body's position and wished him luck. Psycho and Body made plans for Body to collect the money owed on the streets, before he made his move to leave town. They conversed some more and reminisced about old times. Body told Psycho about Tameeka's pregnancy.

"Damn, Ike. What you gonna do bout that?"

"I'm not sure, yet. Honestly, I don't know what to do. I haven't even told her that I'm bouncing."

"Damn, when she finds out that you're moving to ATL, she's gonna be tight." said Psycho.

"Yeah well, she's just gonna have to be tight 'cause I'm out. How do I even know that's my baby, anyway?" said Body. He was trying to convince himself more so than Psycho.

He was looking for a way to turn his back on her. In the pit of his stomach, he knew he was wrong.

"I'm gonna tell her when she comes in tomorrow. I don't wanna do it over the phone."

"Aight, but on another note. When you grab that cash, pick Menace up and take him with you. Make sure the young nigga is straight before you bounce."

"No doubt, my nigga. I'm gonna leave you with this cell phone and hit you up as soon as I hit the streets."

Psycho was feeling sad, but hid his emotions well. Body was like a brother to him. They had literally grown up together. And it was hard for Psycho to imagine him wanting to get out the game and leave him behind. They were building a dynasty together like the city had never seen before. And Body was willing to just walk away from it all. He couldn't understand it. Although, he acted as if he did in Body's presence. He was just hoping it would be temporary like he said.

When Monday morning rolled around Body was already up and prepared to leave for court. He hadn't gotten a wink of sleep the night before. His adrenaline wouldn't allow it. He was too excited at the prospect of going home. His time in the county seemed to fly by, right up until the time his lawyer made him aware of the likelihood of his release. The time seemed to crawl to a standstill. Two weeks felt like two years.

Body shared his plans with Tameeka about relocating to Atlanta and she cried. He managed to shatter her heart once again. She would do anything for him and couldn't understand why he didn't want her. After all the rekindling they've been doing, since he entered the county. Now, he would be released and run out on her. But, he wasn't just running out on *her* this time. He was running out on their child and that hurt most.

Tameeka didn't want to be a single parent and was careful not to get pregnant, until she found a man who possessed the qualities she desired for herself and her children. She was so sure she had found that with Body, but his newest revelations left her feeling like a fool. How could she expect to have a relationship with a man that's incarcerated. She should've listened to her friends who told her it wouldn't work. How could she be so *stupid?*

***

When Body walked into the courtroom, he was sharply dressed in a charcoal gray suit by *Gucci*. He accessorized it with a pink silk tie, and a pair of black *Prada* business shoes. Present in the courtroom for support was Mila, looking as beautiful as ever. Robin, who had gained at least 25 lbs and regained her glow since successfully completing rehab. Jasmine and Mama Jones were also there.

All the women in Body's life were present. He couldn't help, but smile. His lawyer, John Aderman, was present at the defense table shuffling around some legal documents, preparing for the upcoming motion. The court was behind schedule for whatever reason. Proceedings hadn't begun until 10am. Aderman and the DA went back and forth for approximately thirty minutes, spewing legal jargons, before the judge made his decision to dismiss the case. Body was ecstatic. He wasn't able to be released straight from the courtroom like you would see in the movies. He had to go back to the county to be processed, which could take at least another twelve hours.

When he arrived back on the pod, he immediately shared the news with his team. Everyone seemed genuinely happy for him. When they finally called him to be released, they all embraced him, before he went on his way. He didn't take a single item with him when he left.

The only thing he took were the emotional and psychological scars he had accumulated. The humiliation he felt every time some guard said, "Lock the fuck in!". Or made him strip naked, bend at the waist and spread his ass open. He would never forget those things. He was aware of the psychological warfare that the predatory overseers were waging on him and his people. He understood that the war was waged in some of the most subtle ways. He didn't believe it was mere happenstance the mirrors in the cells were made of some dull material and it was impossible to get a clear reflection. Most people believed it was like that for security purposes to keep inmates away from glass. Body figured it was to distort the image that brothas had of themselves. The sad thing was that the tactics *worked*, but not on Body. He was conscious and knowing is half the battle, after all.

Chapter 33

It had been months since Body had his homicide charges dismissed. Psycho, Taliban, and Man Man were preparing for trial. Psycho had pushed, against the advice of his attorney for a speedy trial. He was counting on Jesus to make something happen. But, their scheduled day for trial had arrived and Stickman was still alive and well. Psycho's thoughts were running rampant. He figured since Body was out of jail, already, Jesus may have changed his mind about intervening on their behalf. It was Body who had the baby by his daughter after all. Psycho felt a tightening grip in the pit of his stomach as he sat in the bullpen awaiting to face a once trusted member of his organization. It was the same member who would be responsible for his demise.

The Sheriff's opened the door to the bullpen, cuffed and shackled all three men in preparation to take them upstairs to the courtroom. They walked awkwardly in the uncomfortable shackles. As they made their way down the corridor, they looked like three immaculately dressed ball players on their way to do a press release. The reality of it was that they were walking more of the *Green Mile* than the red carpet.

Coincidently, Judge Henry Hacken was presiding over their case. Cracken Hacken's courtroom was located on the 3rd floor of the building. When they reached the floor they noticed the halls were semi busy with court personnel and other civilians. Psycho didn't see any faces that he recognized, not that he could pay much attention. His mind was focused on the impending trial and how he'd been led astray and played by his connect. *If that nigga didn't wanna be involved, he should've just said so*, Psycho thought. He began clenching his jaws as he moved along, trying to contain his anger. He watched as a female Sheriff exited one of the doors ahead of him. Her back was facing him. Her ass protruded from her uniform pants, threatening to split at the seams. The closer he got to her, the fatter her ass appeared. Then, abruptly she re-entered the room from which she came and ended Psycho's fantasy.

When the three defendants reached Judge Hacken's courtroom, they were escorted inside. Body's presence in the back of the courtroom was the first thing Psycho noticed. He was happy to receive his support. All three men were seated at a long conference table on the right side of the courtroom, reserved for the defense. Once they were seated their shackles and handcuffs were removed. It's state and federal law not to let the jury see a defendant in cuffs because it may prematurely alter their perception.

Psycho's lawyer made him aware that the state would try the case differently. The prosecution would come out swinging hard. First presenting the bulk of the case, then the small circumstantial things surrounding it. His lawyer surmised because Stickman was scheduled to testify that very same day. Usually a Prosecutor would save a witness like Stickman to close out their case. This time would be different. The truth was that the prosecution didn't want to chance that his star witness would get cold feet and back out. He wouldn't allow it to happen. Psycho felt nervousness overcome him. *What if I lose?* He thought. This would be his first time going to trial and it didn't sit well with him that he would have to leave his fate in the hands of twelve strangers, twelve predominately *White* strangers. The jury members were ushered into the courtroom and took their assigned seats.

"All rise, the Honorable Judge Henry Hacken now presides." recited the bailiff. Everyone in the courtroom stood to their feet.

"You may be seated." said the Judge.

After everyone was seated, the DA stepped away from the mound of folders and legal documents on his desk and gave his opening arguments. His opening lasted the better half of two hours. *This guy sure is long winded,* thought Psycho.

After the DA concluded, each attorney of the three defendants had an opportunity to respond to things said by the DA. The men felt like they had the "Dream Team" because all of them had private attorney's.

The District Attorney presented its case by calling the medical examiner to the stand. This was a small nuance of the law, necessary to establish that five people had been murdered. The examiner's testimony took three hours and the defense team opted not to add any further questions. There was no defense they could provide for five dead bodies by attacking the medical examiner.

Next, to hit the stand was the detective who took the key witness' statement. Novak wanted to get his portion of the testimony out of the way because he had a prior engagement to attend. As soon as he was finished on the stand, he exited the courtroom. He felt like he set everything up for Stickman to get the slam dunk.

Judge Hacken called for a ten minute recess while the state prepared it's next witness, which was none other than Stickman.

Psycho looked back into the courtroom and for the first time noticed Detectives Collins. He was on his way out of the courtroom for recess when he smiled at Psycho. He made a frivolous attempt at taunting him.

Probably about to go eat some donuts, fucking pigs, thought Psycho.

After five minutes, the DA was anxiously setting up. Stickman was being escorted into the courtroom by the same female Sheriff that Psycho was crushing on earlier. This time he was able to get a better look at the woman. She had striking features and the prettiest mahogany skin that he had ever seen.

The Sheriff sitting to Psycho's right, raised up and motioned towards the defense table. *Probably to make sure none of us tried to attack Stickman's rat ass,* thought Taliban.

Psycho diverted his attention to Stickman. He was looking down at the floor. He neglected to look in the eyes of those he once called comrade. Psycho looked at the female sheriff, again, unable to take his gaze away from her. Her unbelievable body, small manicured hands, and supermodel swag commanded the attention of the whole room.

Psycho then noticed her hair, which was pinned up into a bun. As he studied it closely, he realized that they were dreadlocks. He began to think intensely about why she seemed so familiar to him. Before, he could come up with an answer his thoughts were interrupted, when she pulled the glock .40 from its holster. She fired two shots at point blank range into Stickman's head as he sat on the witness stand, waiting to give his testimony.

There was another Sheriff assisting her. He quickly made his way in her direction with his government issued glock drawn. He pumped 2 more shots into Stickman's lifeless body, before he and the mysterious woman spun on their heels and exited through the same door from which they came.

The entire courtroom was in pandemonium and screams filled the air. A few jury members returning early from recess dove to the floor in fear. District Attorney, Mark Trolly, cowered underneath the prosecution table wide-eyed in fear. The wet stain in his groin region exposed the fact that he pissed himself. Everyone could see, and he would never live down the embarrassment.

Everything seemed to come back to Psycho at once. She was so beautiful and exotic. Even with the heavy makeup and fake nose it was undeniable. She never told him, exactly, what kind of work she did. He only knew that she worked for Jesus. Naively, he believed she was a model. Now, he knew, exactly, who the mysterious Sheriff lady was. She was Claudia… *and Psycho was in love.*

… to be continued. Resources:

To Book EJ Nunley For speaking, contact hiphoplitpublishing@gmail.com

For the cinematic audio book of Welcome To Steel City,
audiobook.steelcitythebook.com

For the music playlist that accompanies Welcome To Steel City,
music.steelcitythebook.com

If you want to become a published author with
Hip Hop Lit Publishing,
https://www.hiphoplitpublishing.com/contact

CPSIA information can be obtained
at www.ICGtesting.com
Printed in the USA
BVHW041104120521
607049BV00004B/391